SUPER POWERED

TRANSFORM ANXIETY *into* COURAGE, CONFIDENCE, AND RESILIENCE

~ BY ~

RENEE JAIN and Dr. SHEFALI TSABARY

Random House 🏠 New York

Text copyright © 2020 by Renee Jain and Dr. Shefali Tsabary
Cover art copyright © 2020 by Mary Kate McDevitt
Interior illustrations copyright © 2020 by GoStrengths Inc.

Published in the United States by Random House Children's Books,
a division of Penguin Random House LLC, New York.

Random House and the colophon are registered trademarks of
Penguin Random House LLC.

Visit us on the Web! rhcbooks.com

Educators and librarians, for a variety of teaching tools,
visit us at RHTeachersLibrarians.com

Library of Congress Cataloging-in-Publication Data
Names: Tsabary, Shefali, author. | Jain, Renee, author.
Title: Superpowered : transform anxiety into courage, confidence, and resilience /
Dr. Shefali Tsabary, Renee Jain.
Description: First edition. | New York : Random House, [2020] | Includes
bibliographical references and index. | Audience: Ages 8–12 | Audience: Grades 4–6
Summary: "An anti-anxiety toolkit of easy-to-understand methods for recognizing
anxious behaviors and identifying the causes of worried thinking"
—Provided by publisher.
Identifiers: LCCN 2019049376 (print) | LCCN 2019049377 (ebook)
ISBN 978-0-593-12639-4 (hardcover) | ISBN 978-0-593-12641-7 (library binding)
ISBN 978-0-593-12640-0 (epub)
Subjects: LCSH: Security (Psychology) in children—Juvenile literature.
Self-esteem in children—Juvenile literature.
Power (Social sciences)—Juvenile literature.
Classification: LCC BF723.S22 T73 2020 (print) | LCC BF723.S22 (ebook)
DDC 155.4/19—dc23

Printed in the United States of America
10 9 8 7 6 5 4 3 2 1
First Edition

We dedicate this book to our
most powerful teachers: children.
You are now, and always will be,
Superpowered.

CONTENTS

PART THREE: SUPERPOWERED

AUTHORS' NOTE

Psst! One thing before you start. We want you to know that during our careers we've worked with thousands of kids, and each one had amazing stories to share. Some stories made us smile. Some made us cry. But they all taught us something. We feel very strongly that those same stories, the ones shared with us by real kids, can teach you something, too. We've included many in this book, but to protect kids' identities, we've changed names and created new stories by combining or changing the details of their otherwise-real struggles.

Speaking of real struggles, anxiety can be serious and should not be taken lightly. We're about to teach you so much about managing your mental wellness, but nothing we say in this book is intended to substitute for professional medical advice, diagnosis, treatment, and prescribed medication. If you, or a parent or supervising adult, have concerns, questions, or doubts regarding your well-being, please seek medical and/or psychological treatment from a qualified person.

WELCOME!

Oh, you're here! Awesome! We've been waiting for you.

You probably picked up this book because you've been feeling stressed and worried and want help with that. Trust us, you're in the right place and you're going to find more than just a little help.

Inside this book you'll find secrets, strategies, hard truths, science, exercises, and more than a few mind-blowing facts that won't just relieve your worry but will completely transform it. We'll go as far as to say that the journey through this book could change your life. We can't wait for you to dive in. First, here's a bit about us:

I'm Renee Jain (pronounced Ree-knee Jane), and I lived most of my childhood feeling worried about different things: *What if I fail the test? What if no one asks me to the dance? What if I just don't make the team? What if . . .* The list went on. Finally, in my early twenties, I met a counselor who changed my life. He gave me skills I could use to transform my anxiety into power. I made it my life's mission to pass on those skills of resilience to as many kids as possible. I started an organization called GoZen!, where we create programs for kids of all ages to help them live their best lives. As part of this mission, I wrote this book with my dear friend—

Hi. I'm Dr. Shefali! I've always been fascinated with why we think the thoughts we think, feel the feelings we feel, and even do the things we do. In other words, I'm deeply interested in people. That's why I became a clinical psychologist. When kids or adults struggle with their thoughts, feelings, and behavior, they come to me for help. It's been so meaningful to work with families all over the world. Along with Renee, I'm going to take this journey with you, an adventure full of surprises. You're going to learn to relieve your worry, but way beyond that, you're going to learn how to live a *superpowered* life! We created this book as a tool. That means it's going to need to get a little messy if it's going to help you. You'll find exercises throughout most of the chapters, and we hope you write directly on the pages. Yes, we want you to mark it up! Unless, of course, you're borrowing this book from a library, or if you plan on passing it along to someone else when you're done. Then you can use a separate notebook to write out the exercises. We promise, they'll be just as helpful.

Now, what are you waiting for? Go for it!

PART ONE

THE TRUTH

CHAPTER 1
POWER

Sabrina's mom came into her room and opened up the blinds. The sunlight hurt Sabrina's tired eyes. It took her a moment to fully wake up, to remember what was ahead of her that day. But once she did, her anxiety kicked in, her thoughts started to race, and her stomach felt queasy.

She worried about the bus ride. (When her bestie wasn't on the bus, it was hard to figure out who to sit with.) She worried about her math test. (Last week she was moved to the math group that everyone knew was the "extra help" group.) She worried about—

Wait, what did my mom just say? *Sabrina's thoughts often got so loud, she could hardly hear people in the same room with her.*

Her mom repeated: "You need to get this room cleaned up, please. I've already asked about six times this week."

Sabrina looked at her bedroom floor and, sure enough, clothes everywhere. Ugh. So much to do all the time. Wait! She was supposed to wear her soccer jersey to school because there was a game that night. But there it was, wrinkled, dirty, and hanging from the bedpost. Totally unwearable. If she asked her mom to wash it, her mom would get mad. . . . She had a lot to do, too. And

Sabrina didn't even really like to play soccer, which made it all feel worse.

Her stomach hurt. Her head felt like it was underwater. She was hot. It felt like there was a battle inside her body, and she wished everything would just stop.

She didn't remember life being this hard before.

If this book is going to work, we need to be honest with each other. The truth is important. And the truth is that, sometimes, life isn't easy.

Maybe you knew that.

Maybe you knew that because sometimes you have that horrible upset feeling in your stomach, like it's full or burning or about to erupt.

Maybe you knew that because sometimes your thoughts spin like they're on a carnival ride, dizzying, too fast for you to focus, too fast for you to sleep, like hundreds of screams spinning round and round.

Maybe you knew that sometimes life isn't easy, because sometimes you feel worried. Not just worried about things that might be dangerous, but worried about things that are part of a regular day. Worried about going to school. Worried about playing that soccer game. Worried about not being liked. Worried about feeling worried.

When all of those feelings and thoughts swirl together, it's called anxiety.

Anxiety makes us feel nervous, fearful, and terribly

insecure. Anxiety makes us feel like running away and hiding, and sometimes we really do. Anxiety makes us feel like yelling and screaming, and sometimes we really do. Anxiety makes us feel like not trying anymore, and sometimes—well, you get the point.

There you go. That's the cold, hard truth. But that's not the *whole* truth. There's *more*. And believe us, you're going to want to hear this *more*.

Anxiety doesn't need to feel so awful.

There are ways to transform anxiety so that it actually works for you.

The first step in learning how to deal with anxiety is to understand *why* we're anxious. The moment we can figure this out, the rest takes care of itself. So, why are we so anxious? Time for another truth: the main reason we're all anxious is because our *superpowers* have been zapped.

Are you rolling your eyes because we're talking about superpowers? Hold on. We're not saying you have super-strength, laser vision, and that you secretly battle villains at night (although that would be cool). We're saying that if you're reading this (we're pretty sure you are), and if you're human (again, pretty sure that's true), then you have a special set of powers that can supercharge you through life and help you fight stress, worry, and pressure. The problem? No one told you that you had these powers or how to use them.

That's where we come in. We've worked with thousands of kids, each one unique, and every single one—without exception—has these skills we call superpowers. These super-powers are hidden deep within us. Sometimes they feel totally nonexistent, but they're definitely there. Every single one of us came into this world fully charged with five incredible super-powers.

Your Five Incredible Superpowers!

SUPERPOWER #1: You were an explorer! There was a time when you couldn't take a walk without touching the grass, smelling flowers, listening to the buzz of bees, tasting rain-drops, and just watching . . . everything. You wanted to be part of it all. But it wasn't just stuff on the outside; you paid atten-tion to what was inside you. You had really BIG feelings, and whether you were happy, worried, sad, or angry, you weren't afraid to feel and express those feelings. If you felt sad, you'd cry. If you were happy, you'd smile. Like all explorers, you came into the world with the incredible superpower of being **Present**!

SUPERPOWER #2: You were true to you! While grown-ups may have dressed you in cute, color-coordinated outfits, you thought wearing mismatched socks and your pajamas to school was a great idea. If you wanted to sing at the top of your lungs, you did so without caring if you sounded terrible or not. In other words, you did whatever felt good *to you* and didn't care a bit what anyone thought. You weren't born to follow rules. You played with toys that interested you, no matter what was popular. You ate foods you were curious about, however "gross" the combination. You made up words, had imaginary friends, and laughed at your own jokes. You were busy discovering all the unique things that make you who you are. You embraced being **Original**!

SUPERPOWER #3: There was a time in your life when you truly loved yourself. You looked in the mirror and adored the person who looked back at you. When you took a test, you didn't fall apart if you got a bad grade. And when you didn't score the winning goal, you didn't sulk for days. You simply felt good about yourself, regardless of how you performed, how you looked, or what others thought about you. No matter what, you were proud and couldn't wait to show off your accomplishments. You had a powerful sense of inner worth, and incredible character

strengths that made you unique. You felt **Whole**!

SUPERPOWER #4: You loved life! There was a time when you jumped out of bed every morning ready to take on the world. "What are we doing today?!" you'd shout. Each day was an endless source of adventure and joy. New things were exciting, and no one had to convince you that learning was fun. You were always on the go, looking for new things to spark your curiosity and ignite your imagination. Sometimes your energy got you into trouble, but you didn't mind. Life was too much of an adventure! In fact, you had to be convinced you were tired and needed rest. Your curiosity was all the motivation and entertainment you needed. You had the superpower of being **Energized**!

SUPERPOWER #5: You were a risk taker! When you first started to walk, it wasn't easy. You fell down hundreds of times, but never gave up, because you never thought that FALLING meant FAILING. Falling was just part of the learning process. You approached everything this way—learning to eat by yourself, getting dressed on your own, brushing your teeth, riding a bike. It didn't matter how messy or clumsy you were. You never gave up on things until you mastered them. You were born knowing how to overcome challenges and take risks. You were born **Resilient**!

There you have it. You came into this world with five superpowers. Want a recap?

PRESENT

ORIGINAL

WHOLE

ENERGIZED

RESILIENT

POWER. It's an acronym. As you'll see, we like acronyms!

Here's the thing: somehow, as you started growing up, these superpowers got thwacked, bonked, fizzled, blanked, vanished, faded . . . *zapped!* Basically, as you grew up, little by little, you began to forget about your powers, and each time a power was zapped, it was replaced by something else: worry, anxiety, and all sorts of other little thoughts that make you feel anything but superpowered. Zapped powers can transform a life full of passion and adventure into one of challenges and struggle. If you picked up this book, you've probably felt this struggle. We have, too. So, we're going to ask you for one thing—your trust. Trust the process of this book. You'll learn exactly what happened to your superpowers as well as the exact steps to get them back. Each chapter will help you make small changes that eventually lead to big transformation!

- Life isn't always easy, and that's okay. Most people feel anxious and uncomfortable sometimes.

- You were born with the powers to be **Present, Original, Whole, Energized,** and **Resilient.** You may not feel those powers right now, but you're going to get them back!

PRESENT

RES

You fail as an important part of growth and learning

You are an explorer of each moment. You get power from the here and now.

ORIGINAL

You show up as your authentic, rad, true self in every situation.

ILIENT
You thrive on curiosity and innovation.
ENERGIZED
You are worthy and full of strengths just as you are.
WHOLE
super
POWER

CHAPTER 2
ZAPPED!

Kellen's orchestra concert was a whole week away, but it was all he could think about. Things he used to love (baseball practice, ice cream after dinner, YouTube) were all background noise now, as if worrying about this concert were his purpose on this earth and everything else was a distraction. The concert was on his mind all day, and it kept him up at night.

Thing is, this was his third concert, and each time the worry seemed to get worse. He worried about little things, like what to wear. His favorite pants were yellow, but NOBODY else ever wore yellow pants. He worried that he'd mess up his solo, that he'd miss notes or cues and everyone would know he wasn't that good. He worried that he no longer measured up compared to the other cellists. All these things totally wrecked his motivation to practice, and the less he practiced, the more he had to worry about.

He didn't remember life being this hard before.

We've had so many conversations with so many kids that it's easy to imagine what many of you want to say to us: "If our superpowers were really that super to begin with, how'd they get zapped? What good are these powers if they can be

defeated so easily? You said 'challenges and struggles.' That's putting it mildly! I mean, we're talking about some pretty strong, painful emotions here."

Believe us, we understand that you may be skeptical. And yes, we know how overwhelming anxiety can be. That's why we're here, to help you remember your powers so you can fight back once again. In order to use your powers to fight worry, you need to understand exactly what you're up against. Let's take a closer look at what happens when your super-powers are replaced.

ZAPPED: From Present to What-iffing

When you used your superpower of being **Present** as a kid, you were always interested in what was happening in that very moment. If there was a storm, or a sunset, or a squirrel in your yard, you watched it all. Your mind was here and now. You weren't thinking about your test the next day or about what your friend had said weeks before. You were totally, fully, completely **Present,** and being **Present** allowed you to experience life joyfully.

Things began to change when your superpower of being **Present** got zapped! You stopped being in the present moment, and instead your thoughts began to time-travel. Your mind wandered into the past—worrying about things you'd said or done days, or even weeks, before. Or your mind wandered into the future—worrying about things that hadn't happened yet, or might never even happen!

Time traveling might be fun in the movies, but in real life it's a serious worry-maker. When time-traveling worries invade, we call it What-iffing, and when it happens to you, it sounds something like this: *What if I don't get good grades? What if I said the wrong thing to my friend yesterday? What if I mess up my speech tomorrow? What if I don't know what to be when I grow up?*

What-iffing creates so much stress and pain because it makes us forget where we are and makes us afraid of where we aren't.

ZAPPED: From Original to Camouflaged

When you were using all your superpowers, you embraced being a complete **Original**! You felt free to say what was on your mind and do as you pleased. You weren't scared of other people's opinions and couldn't have cared less if they approved

of you or not. But guess what happened? Your power got zapped, and you began to care about what others thought about you—a lot.

You started changing parts of yourself to fit in. You hid your real feelings and opinions. You started dressing in outfits and acting in ways you never would have if you were truly being yourself. You started trying to blend in with everyone around you. You started changing your image on social media, hoping to get more followers and likes. You began to Camouflage. And while hiding your true self didn't feel good, you figured out how to mask that pain, too. When you Camouflage, you think things like: *What will everyone else be wearing? I can't admit I like this song if nobody else does. How do I get my hair to look just like hers? If I post this on social media, will people like me? How do I get everyone to notice me? Why can't I just fit in?*

One day you were being you, and the next day you were trying to be someone else, all because it felt important to fit in. Your friends and family and what they thought of you mattered more than what you thought about yourself. And when you change yourself to get others' approval, it's really hard to ever feel good about yourself.

ZAPPED: From Whole to Cocooned

Remember what it was like to always love yourself? When you were using the superpower of being **Whole,** you felt confident, proud, and perfect in your abilities. Every picture you drew, you hung on the refrigerator. Every song you sang was loud enough for all to hear. If you did color outside the lines, sing out of tune, or give a wrong answer, it didn't matter one bit. You still felt **Whole.** You knew you were still totally amazing.

But then you noticed that people really judged things, like grades and trophies. They didn't seem to care about what you loved to do, as much as they cared about how good you were at doing it. Slowly the worry, the doubt, and the anxiety began to creep in. When your superpower of feeling **Whole** got zapped, you started to feel like who you were depended on what you did. Instead of feeling confident in who you were, you felt like you weren't good enough. You judged yourself based on numbers like grades, test scores, how many goals you scored, how many likes you got on social media, how many people came to your birthday party. All of this made you feel vulnerable, hurt your confidence, and damaged your belief in yourself, until you began to protect your image. You began to Cocoon yourself and stopped taking chances, in order to avoid being criticized.

When you're **Whole,** everything you need is inside you. When you

Cocoon yourself, no one sees the beauty on the inside. Your thoughts echo this insecurity, and they sound something like this: *I'm not smart enough to do that. No matter how hard I try, nothing I ever do is good enough. I don't like myself very much, and nobody else does, either.*

ZAPPED: From Energized to Fried

When you were **Energized,** nobody needed to tell you what to do. No alarm needed to wake you up. No adults needed to tell you to hurry. No coaches needed to tell you to run. You did things on your own because you were motivated. You "felt like it." You were **Energized** by life! How many things still make you feel like that?

When your superpower of being **Energized** got zapped, you felt exhausted . . . ALL. THE. TIME. As you began to feel pressure from people who were always telling you how to be and when to be, you lost your own motivation to learn. Instead of using your own curiosity and excitement to drive you, you forced yourself to move forward. You began to feel overwhelmed, behind schedule, tired, and like you never had enough time to do the things that really interested you. You felt overworked. Overscheduled. Over-EVERYTHINGed. We call this feeling Fried.

It used to be mostly adults who felt Fried. Believe us, we've felt Fried a lot. But more and more kids are coming to us all the time with zapped energy. They're Fried, too, and to them, nothing feels worth their effort. They think and feel things that

PIANO LESSONS BASEBALL HOMEWORK

sound like this: *I'm too tired. I'd rather just stay home and hang out. I have way too much to do, and I don't have any time to just do my own thing or have fun. I'm so sick of going to practice. . . . It's, like, all I ever do!*

ZAPPED: From Resilient to Iced

Being **Resilient** means being able to bounce back from a challenge, and it's a superpower we were all born with. We fell down, and we got back up again. We totally messed up, we got over it, and we tried again.

Over and over. It's how we learned. But somehow we forgot that. The idea of a mistake started to make us feel useless, like we couldn't do anything right. Yup, that's right. We got zapped again.

When your superpower of being **Resilient** got zapped, you felt stuck. You hesitated to try out for teams, answer questions in class, or meet new people. When you felt even the slightest possibility of failure, you worried about putting yourself out there. In fact, some of us are so freaked out by mistakes that we won't try new things unless we're guaranteed 100 percent success. And when you don't try new things, you can't grow as a person. You're frozen.

If this feels familiar, you're Iced, and your thoughts look like this: *I want to try out for the swim team, but I know I'm not that great, so what's the point of signing up? I want to go out with my friends, but I'll just get left out, so I'd better stay home. I only got six out of ten correct on my math test. . . . Next time I'm not even going to try.*

Okay, that was a lot of info! Here's a quick recap of what it looks like to go from superpowered to zapped.

Feel like you've lost some of your superpowers? Great! Well, not great that you feel like you lost them, but great that you're reading this, because there's another truth you need to know: superpowers are *never* truly lost . . . only zapped! All of them are still right there within you, just hidden from sight. We wrote this book to show you exactly what you need to do to reveal and reactivate your superpowers, step by step.

- Your superpowers of being **Present**, **Original**, **Whole**, **Energized**, and **Resilient** have been zapped and replaced by What-iffing, Camouflaging, Cocooning, and being Fried and Iced.

CHAPTER 3
SHOULDED

Now we're getting somewhere. Let's look at what you've learned so far: you were born with superpowers, but your powers may have been zapped and replaced with worries, fears, anxieties, insecurities, and other difficult emotions. How did this even happen? Here's the straightest answer we can give: you got *shoulded*.

Shoulded? Iced? What-iffing? If it sounds like we're making words up, well, we kind of are. We're embracing our superpower of being **Original.**

Let us explain what it means to get shoulded. Have you ever followed instructions for putting together a model? Or followed a recipe for making a meal? Or some other list of things you "should" do if you want something to come out "right"? Well, shoulds are like instructions for people. Nobody is really sure where these instructions came from, but they clearly exist.

If any of this sounds familiar, then you're being shoulded around.

Now, it's not as if your parents, teachers, classmates—

You should get good grades.

You should be happy.

You should work to your potential.

You should be kind.

You should try hard.

You should make lots of friends.

okay, basically all humans—are telling you that you should constantly do things because everyone is mean. Quite the opposite. Getting shoulded often happens out of love and respect, and really, in the right context, it's not bad advice, right? Should you try to get good grades? Well, sure. Should you try to work hard? Yup! Everyone who loves you wants you to grow up and be the best possible version of yourself, so they tell you what they think you should do to make that happen.

The problem comes when getting shoulded doesn't inspire

you to reach goals and instead makes you feel like you need to be someone other than who you are right now. Every time you hear about what you should do, you feel like you aren't measuring up, and you aren't good enough. And that's when your superpowers get zapped!

Let's meet some real kids who have been shoulded. In some cases, you'll notice how the shoulds came from a place of love and concern, even though they may have caused hurt.

"YOU SHOULD BE HAPPY!"

Anna worries. She worries about her grades and what people think of her, and she worries about how much she worries. At night she gets quiet and sad, and sometimes cries. When her parents see her upset, they get upset, and that's the absolute worst, because then not only is she sad, but she's the reason why other people are sad, too, like she's some cloud that just rains on everybody. Her parents want her to be grateful for having a nice house and a loving family. They always remind her that she should be happy, like it's some switch she can flip on. Being told she should be happy makes her feel broken. Turns out it's way easier just to hide all her feelings. So she becomes even more quiet and more withdrawn. What if she never figures out this happiness thing? More things to worry about.

"YOU SHOULD BE MORE SOCIAL!"

Bandile is often called shy, but he hates that word. It makes him picture little kids hiding behind their parents' legs, but he's in eighth grade now. He often eats lunch alone and rarely hangs out after school. His dad is always nagging him to be more outgoing and social, "just like I was at that age." His mom pushes him to sign up for all sorts of activities, hoping he'll make friends. But the more they push him, the more nervous and unsure of himself he gets. He thinks, *Maybe there really is something wrong with me.*

"YOU SHOULD WORK TO YOUR POTENTIAL!"

Gracie does well enough at school, gets average grades, and balances her academics with an active social life. What she really loves are her friends, hobbies, pets . . . basically, having fun.

While Gracie is comfortable being an average student, her parents are definitely not. They always push her to work harder. Study more. Focus better. They keep telling her that she needs to work to her potential. She must have heard that word a thousand times. Potential, potential, potential. Gracie is so sick of her parents telling her to work more that she actually wants to work less. What used to come naturally to her now feels like a chore. If she used to have any passion for working hard, it's totally gone now.

Yeah, being shoulded doesn't feel good. And to think, these are just a few of the thousands of stories we've heard. (We haven't even mentioned our own shoulding stories.) What are some ways you have been shoulded around? Think about it, and take some time to share.

This is how I am naturally:

_____

_____

_____

_____

_____

_____

_____

This is how I've been shoulded to be:

_____

_____

_____

_____

_____

_____

_____

This is how being shoulded makes me feel:

_____

_____

_____

_____

_____

_____

Before we move on, we need to make sure we're clear about something. We're not saying that you shouldn't listen to advice, especially advice from people who love you. We all want to be our best selves, and the people who care about us most want to help us do that. There is a big difference between getting shoulded (which can make us feel bad about who we are) and learning from others or setting goals for ourselves. So getting shoulded isn't all bad. The problem is when we think we should listen to others or we'll risk losing their love or approval. The trick is to listen without letting the suggestions overwhelm what we feel is natural and right for us. Not easy, right?

We get it! That's why we're giving you the tools to empower yourself. You'll be able to figure out what's right for you and not simply follow others' shoulds because you feel . . . you should. You're going to have the tools to transform your worry, love the person you are today, and feel inspired—not exhausted—by your goals.

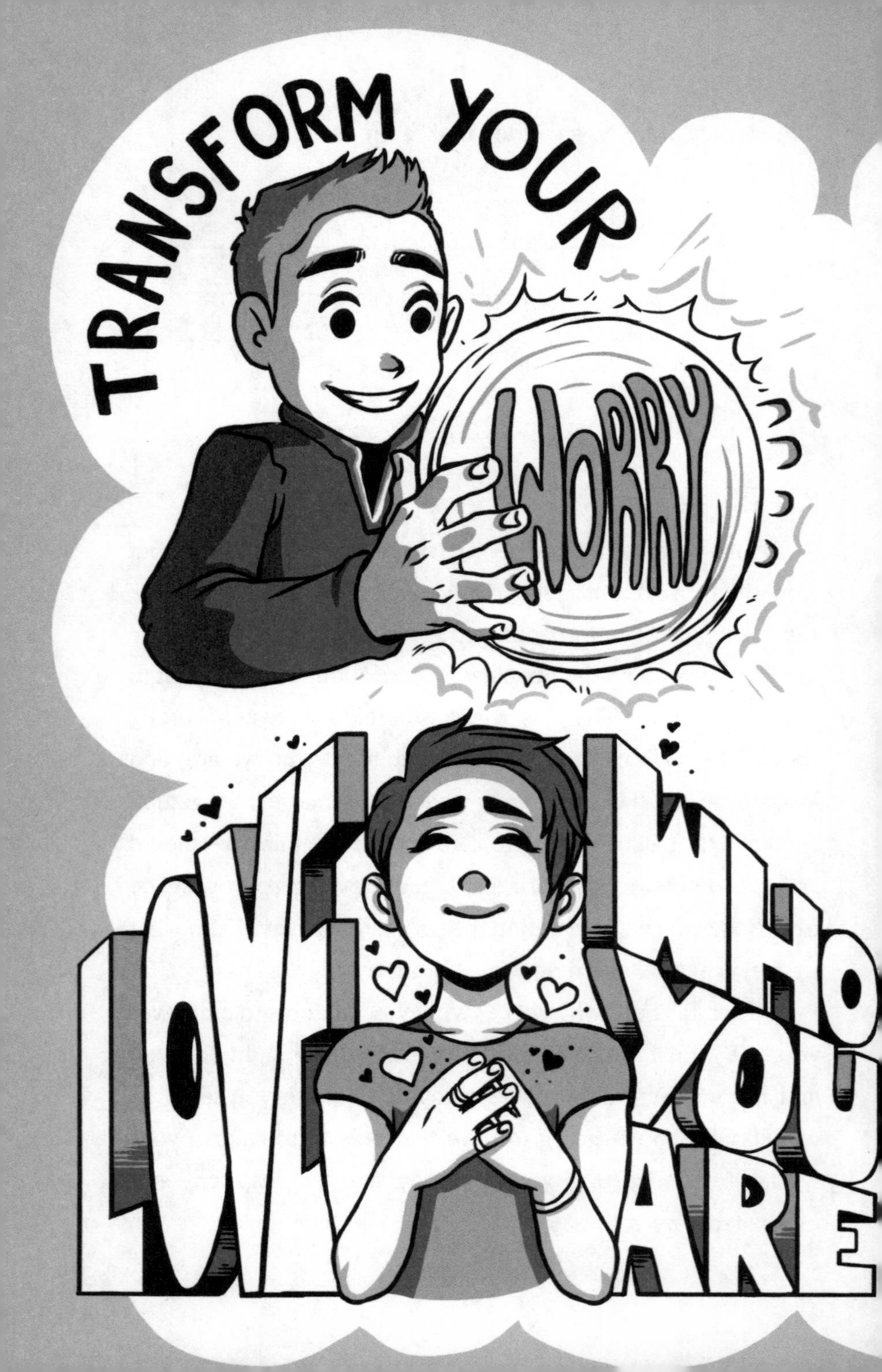
TRANSFORM YOUR
WORRY
LOVE
WHO
YOU
ARE

Try these exercises!

1. How do you feel shoulded in your life? Write some "should" statements on the hands below.

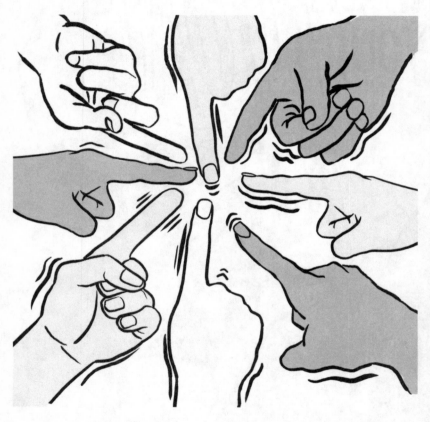

2. How do you should others in your life? Do you sometimes should friends, siblings, or even your parents? We all do it some of the time, and it's great to be aware of our shoulding habits. Next, write in some "should" statements you've made to others.

KEY TAKEAWAYS

- When we are told, or made to feel, that we're supposed to be doing something differently than we are, we call it being shoulded.

- Being shoulded, while often done out of love or concern, can make us feel like we're not good enough or doing enough, and opens the door to our feeling worried and anxious.

CHAPTER 4
THE MESSENGER

The Worry Nobody Can See
My hands start to sweat,
My legs start to shake,
My tummy starts to turn,
My heart starts to ache,
My head starts to spin,
My breathing gets faster,
I know what will happen,
If I don't obey my master.
These are some of the feelings inside
I get when anxiety takes over the ride.
I try to control it but never succeed.
I wish someone would give me
the cuddle I need.

—Maddison, age 11

It has always amazed us how worry-thoughts can show up as worry-pains in the body. You know those moments when you're anxious about a test, a project, or a birthday party, and

suddenly BAM! your body strikes back? If you try to explain this to someone who has never felt this, they don't really get it. They think, *Come on. It can't be that bad, right?* If they only knew that what was going on inside you was like a battle: blasts that cause body aches, headaches, and stomachaches; clashes that cause nausea and shortness of breath; shocks that make you bite your fingernails; screams in your brain that keep you awake at night. It's a battle as big as any you've seen in the movies!

What does your body feel like when you get really worried? Circle what you feel:

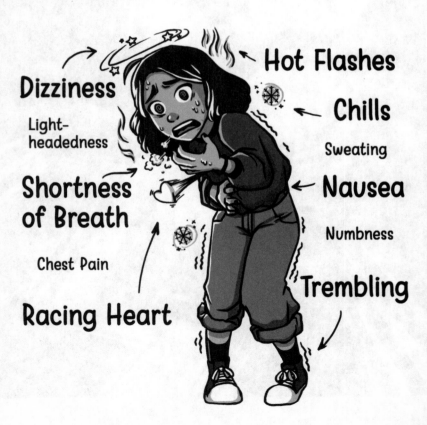

Dizziness

Light-headedness

Shortness of Breath

Chest Pain

Racing Heart

Hot Flashes

Chills

Sweating

Nausea

Numbness

Trembling

Maybe you don't know exactly how to describe what happens when you feel worried. You just know *it feels bad*. You're not alone. In fact, millions of humans of all ages have experienced intense worry and the physical pain that goes with it, and they would do whatever it takes to make it go away. That's right. Millions of people feel just like you (maybe even hundreds of millions).

Have you had enough of our chatting yet? Are you saying to yourself, *Just tell me already! HOW do I use my powers to get rid of this worry?!*

Here comes a big truth alert:

You don't get rid of worry.

Wait! Don't throw the book down! We're going to help you with the difficult feelings, repetitive thoughts, and much more, but, believe it or not, getting rid of worry altogether would be worse than any bad experience you've had with it. Here are the facts, according to science:

Worry has a purpose. Worry has benefits. Worry is *good* for you.

Worry and the Cave Person

Let's zip back a few hundred thousand years to the time of cave people. Imagine a cave person running barefoot, spear in hand, looking to capture her next meal. Can you picture it? Suddenly a saber-toothed cat attacks! The moment the cave person senses danger, her brain sends a "worry message" to her body. Her body receives the message and makes quick changes: the heart races to send blood to muscles; functions such as digesting food are shut down so she can save energy; her thoughts speed up so she can think fast; breathing gets deeper and faster so she has more oxygen in case she needs to run far and fast. Amazing, right?

Scientists call this the fight, flight, or freeze response. We call it the 3Fs for short. The 3Fs make the body stronger, faster, and focused on danger. Worry helped the cave person. The cave person *needed* worry in order to survive.

Why We Need Worry Today

We're guessing that you don't get chased by any prehistoric animals on the way to school, so why would you need worry to protect you? Even in your modern-day life, there are dangers, and worry still has a place. When you're about to touch a hot stove, worry sends a message and tells your body to yank your hand away. Worry sends messages to protect you from stepping into traffic, talking to strangers, or swimming too far from shore. And, get this! Worry has continued to change over time. It has evolved to send different kinds of messages and produce different kinds of responses in your body, depending on the situation. For example, you don't necessarily go into fight, flight, or freeze when giving a speech, taking a test, or pitching in the big game. Instead you may experience something called the challenge response, which can help you perform better!

FIGHT

FLIGHT

FREEZE

There's more to come on that soon. For now, here's a recap:

Worry = Helpful = Good for You!

Unfortunately, you've probably also noticed that worry sometimes sends messages even when there isn't any real danger, like when you're talking to a friend, or just trying to get to sleep at night. We call those messages "brain spam," like junk mail, and we'll also talk more about how to handle that in just a bit.

For now, let's get back to the question that started this chapter: If worry is so good, why does it *feel* so bad? The problem is not the feeling itself; it's the way we *think* about the feeling that causes us to feel so awful. We usually think about worry as being bad or scary. *Thinking* that your worried feelings are scary actually creates fear and discomfort inside your mind and body. If you think worry is bad for you, then when you worry, it feels scary in the moment, and also later on when you think back, you might feel worried again. It can be a never-ending worry loop!

So, if the way we think about feelings isn't helpful for us, what's a *better* way to think about them? We want you to think about your feelings as *messengers*. Each feeling (even worry) contains important information. You just need to receive the message and understand what it's saying.

Meet the Messenger

You may have noticed that we've started talking about worry like she's a person. We want you to do exactly the same thing. No matter what age you are, giving worry a name, a face, and an attitude helps you to see worry as a friend instead of an enemy. To help you with this, we created Wisteria the Worrier. We call her Wisty for short. She's strong and fiercely protective, and she uses her unique communication system to send us worry messages.

Wisty's job is to protect us from danger, to set our body into motion when we need to get to safety, and even to motivate us when we need to perform (like on a test or when we're meeting someone new). But sometimes Wisty gets it wrong. Sometimes she sends us worry messages when there is no danger or we don't need a boost of energy or motivation. Sometimes we try to ignore the worry messages and the feelings in our body, and she sends more messages. This is why it's important for us to have a relationship with Wisty—we need to be able to talk back to her!

WISTERIA the WORRIER

Visualizing your worry as Wisty changes your relationship with worry. You start to see worry as someone you can talk to and not someone you need to fear. If you like Wisty, then use her as your worry character. Otherwise, feel free to create your own! What does your worrier look like? What's their name? Do they look like a person? An animal? Are they strong and powerful? Are they wise and quick? Use this space to show us what your worrier looks like:

Talk to Wisty

Now that you have your worry character—either Wisty or your own version—what do you do? Time to start talking to them. You can do this using three steps: Expect, Allow, and Talk Back. (Wait. Are we actually asking you to talk out loud to a fictional character that represents your worry? Yes, that is exactly what we're asking you to do. We've worked with people ages four to seventy-four, and this technique is powerful at any age!)

1. Expect Wisty. You probably already know that you worry about a lot of the same kinds of things or at the same times of day. That means Wisty is kind of predictable. Maybe she sends worry messages before a big event, at bedtime, before school, or when you try something new. If Wisty makes you worry in predictable ways, then you can expect her before she comes, and you can plan what to do.

In which other situations/times can you predict Wisty?

What times of day does Wisty show up?

In what common situations do you encounter Wisty?

2. Allow Wisty in. If you've been scared of feeling worried, then you've probably been trying to make your worry go away by distracting yourself or somehow avoiding your worry. What do you usually do when Wisty shows up? What do you usually do when you worry?

_____

_____

_____

_____

_____

_____

_____

_____

It's time to allow Wisty in. This means that the next time you worry, you're not going to run from it or try to make it go away. When you ignore Wisty, she just keeps sending worry to your body. Next time you worry, say something like this out loud (repeat these statements out loud now for practice):

Hey, Wisty, I see you're making me worry.

Wisty, I think you're trying to tell me something. I feel my heart beating fast, so I know you're sending me messages.

Wisty, is that you again? Okay, I was expecting you.... Go ahead and do your thing.

3. Talk back to Wisty. Wisty—your feelings of worry—is communicating with you, but sometimes she gets it wrong. Wisty can send you messages, but she's not in charge of what you do. You are in charge of you! If Wisty is getting it wrong, it's time to tell her. Talking back to Wisty helps put your logical brain back in charge. On the next two pages are some examples of talking back to Wisty. In the blanks, write down what you're going to say the next time she shows up.

Decode Wisty's Messages

Since we've worked with lots of kids, we've figured out that Wisty sends a lot of the same types of messages. These messages are usually sent directly to your body, so they're in secret code, but we've cracked the code for you. Here are the four most common messages from Wisty, what they mean, and what to do in each case. (By the way, three out of the four types of messages from Wisty are actually helpful!)

Message Type #1: BLAZE

When do you get the Blaze message?

Dangerous situations, fires, walking in parking lots, crossing streets, getting lost, touching something too hot or too cold

What Wisty is trying to say: "You're in real danger! I'm activating the 3Fs to help you run away and survive!"

Benefits: Protection, survival

Action: Listen to Wisty and get to safety!

Reflect: Can you remember a time when you received a Blaze message?

Message Type #2: CHALLENGE

When do you get the Challenge message? Before tests, speeches, performances, and social events

What Wisty is trying to say: "You're facing a challenge and you need motivation, focus, and energy. I can help with those things!"

Benefits: Motivation, productivity, creativity

Action: Wisty is actually working to help you, so use the energy she is sending to your advantage. Jump from worry to excitement before a test or performance by saying phrases like "I am excited!" or "These feelings I have are helping me perform better." (You're going to get more practice with this later in the book.)

Reflect: Does Wisty show up for you before you have to speak in front of crowds or take tests?

Message Type #3: CONNECT

When do you get the Connect message? When you're feeling socially alone, when your feelings have been badly hurt

What Wisty is trying to say: "You're not alone in this. I'm trying to send a message to your body that you need to connect with someone you care about and love who can help support you through this."

Benefits: Social support

Action: Reach out to someone you trust and tell them you want to share something with them.

Reflect: Who do you connect with when you're worried?

Message Type #4: SPAM

When do you get the Spam message? When thinking about the past or the future, at random times

What Wisty is trying to say: "Spam! Spam! Spam! I'm feeling overprotective and maybe even confused. I'm sending you this message and making your body worry, but I'm not sure you need it."

Benefits: None, except that you learn how to identify and deal with brain spam

Action: Let the thoughts float by. Thank Wisty and let her know that she's sending you brain spam, and you're putting it into your "junk box."

Reflect: Does Wisty send you brain spam?

Decode your messages!

Time to decode your messages from Wisty. Write down a few worried thoughts, what type of message each one is, and what action you can take:

Message from Wisty (worried thought)	Type: Blaze, Challenge, Connect, Spam	Action
This speech is making me nervous.	challenge	This worry is helping me prepare for this speech. I am excited!

- Worry is a good thing, and we should never try to get rid of it altogether.

- Worry is a message from our brain that's trying to protect us, and we'd be in a lot of trouble without it.

- Worry communicates with us in different ways, and by decoding the messages, we can learn to change our relationship—and even make friends—with worry.

PART TWO

SHED THE SHOULDS

Congratulations! You've taken your first step toward regaining your superpowers. You now know what your powers are and how you lost them. You know the different ways we worry, and how the shoulds made those worries so strong that they overtook your powers. And you've also learned that we need to get worry back on our side. We need her as an ally to survive, and the sooner we can shed the shoulds and get worry focused on real dangers, the sooner we can focus our energy on becoming superpowered.

In part two of this book, we'll help you do just that: learn to recognize and control each of your power-zapping worries!

CHAPTER 5
WHAT-IFFING

Luna's Journal
March 8, 4:53 a.m.

seriously? I'm up way before
my alarm again. I wish I could just
go back to sleep, but I have that
feeling like I'm about to throw up.

I probably won't actually do it. . . .
I'll just have that disgusting
sick feeling all day. That's what
happened last time, and just
thinking about it makes me feel
nauseated again. speaking of
being sick . . . fractions. I can't
stop thinking about them. The
math test is today and fractions
always mess me up. Like, EVERY
TIME! what if there are fractions

on the test again? What if I
didn't study enough? What if I
don't get an A? What if I have to
go to tutoring? What if I don't
get better and I fail? What if
this affects what college I can
get into? What if I can't stop my
thoughts? What if . . .

At any moment we can drive forward into the future or hit reverse and go into the past. How? With our amazing minds. You've experienced this before: one minute you're in class with your mind on the lesson, and then suddenly your thoughts race forward in time to Friday's soccer tryouts. Then, in the very next second, they turn around and go backward to a memory of the first day of school. Then they speed forward again to that party you got invited to. All that zipping and zooming in time can happen within seconds, and we do it constantly. In fact, according to scientific studies, nearly half our time is spent thinking about things in our past or in our future.

Time traveling allows us to do all sorts of great things, but if we aren't careful, we can easily become stuck in the past or future. We're often powerless to get back to the present moment, and lots of worry is caused by being stuck in the past or the future.

Reliving the Past

Our brains are powerful recorders. They not only capture pictures and sounds, but they can record tastes, smells, and physical sensations as well. Let's say you're thinking about how anxious you were getting on the school bus last week. When you think about it, you might feel like you can still hear the laughs and screams from the other kids, still smell the exhaust from outside the bus, and even feel the horrible nausea from worrying about where you were going to sit. With all your senses reactivated, a worry-thought from the past can make you *feel* a worry-pain in the present.

Which of *your* senses activate when you feel worried about something from the past?

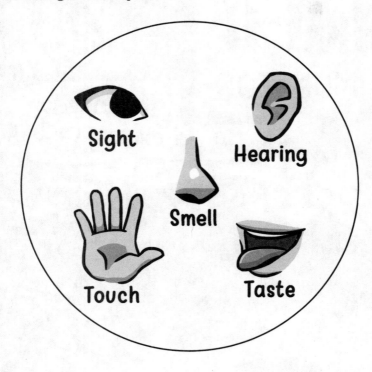

Reliving worry from the past is not fun, but, like with all worry, there's a reason for it. We're supposed to vividly re-member past mistakes so that we can learn from them. That way, we're less likely to repeat them in the future. But the real problem starts when your own personal time machine—your mind—can't figure out how to bring you back into the present. Your mind just plays the bad memory on a loop, and you expe-rience the same worry, over and over, even when you're no longer learning from the experience.

Math test tomorrow!
Then I'll set a Reminder.
WHAT IF I FORGET TO STUDY?
Then I'll make an escape plan with my family.
WHAT IF THERE'S A FIRE?
Just in case of a fire...
WHAT IF I GET A SOLO PART?
I'll take my instrument home to practice.
Concert next week?

Preparing for the Future

Humans are typically considered the only species on Earth that can think ahead and make complex plans for the future. Thinking about the future has a lot of benefits, including helping us with decision-making, motivating us to reach goals, and allowing us to plan for emergencies. You think about the future constantly. You schedule time to do homework. You practice so you're ready for the game. You make a family plan in case of a fire. It's a skill you'll use your whole life, maybe even more when you're an adult!

Airplane pilots, for example, have to know how to handle certain situations. What if a bird hits the plane? What if an engine fails? What if lightning strikes the plane? When learning, pilots don't just read a book and take a written test. They actually get into a flight simulator—a virtual reality machine that gets them as close to the real flying experience as possible—and face dangerous situations to see what they'll do. The pilots practice *how to react* to future challenges.

Your brain does the same thing. It has a simulation feature that thinks about all of the possible futures and asks what-if questions to practice what to do in challenging situations. Your brain asks the questions, hoping to get a response like this: "*If* that challenge comes up, *then* I'll do this." Your brain is making plans. It's almost like practicing life before it happens!

We know from scientists that worrying makes it harder for the logical part of your brain to think clearly—the part responsible for planning, organization, and decision-making. So, your brain still tries to simulate the future and asks what-if questions. But if you're worrying instead of creating plans, your brain can get stuck in a long loop of what-if questions. As we said earlier, we call this What-iffing. This is what happened to Luna, who was thinking about her future at the beginning of this chapter.

If you've been worrying a lot, you've probably been What-iffing. If you've been What-iffing, you already know that it's really hard to stop. One of the problems with stopping is that the plans that feel like they should totally stop your worrying . . . usually completely FAIL. To help, we've made a list of the top three things that make What-iffing worse:

FAIL #1: Squishing. Pushing the thoughts out of your mind or pretending they don't exist are all forms of thought squishing, and it doesn't work. (True story: scientists call this

thought suppression, but we like squishing better!) Do you do this to your thoughts sometimes? Does it work?

FAIL #2: Pacifying. If parents, teachers, or anyone else tells you that "everything is going to be okay," it's called reassurance. If you're stuck What-iffing and grown-ups do this to you, it's because they care. However, while you may feel better for a few minutes, it usually doesn't stop the What-iffing. Do your parents or friends try to pacify you sometimes? How does it feel?

FAIL #3: Bullying. Getting mad at yourself for What-iffing is like kicking yourself when you're down. It feels terrible, and it also doesn't help the What-iffing go away. Do you feel you have an inner bully? What does your bully look like? What does it say to you?

So, now that you know what not to do when it comes to What-iffing, we're going to give you some strategies that do work.

Try these exercises!

1. **Stop the What-iffing dominoes.** When one what-if question tips into another, and another, and eventually spirals into a disastrous story in your mind, you've got a case of the dominoes! The mind sometimes creates stories that are exaggerated and unrealistic. It's time to take your power back by reeling in your thoughts and creating more realistic endings to the story.

    Unrealistic: *What if I do poorly on the test? → What if I fail the class? → What if I don't get into college? → What if I don't get a good job?*

    More realistic: *What if I do poorly on the test? → I'll have to study harder or get a tutor. → My grade might be affected, but that's something I can handle. → I'll remember that grades are feedback on things I'm still learning. If I feel bad about it, that's okay; the feeling will pass.*

   Your turn! Try turning your unrealistic stories into more realistic ones—put your What-iffing thoughts in the tops of the dominoes and your Present thoughts in the bottoms:

76

STOP the DOMINOES

UNREALISTIC

REALISTIC

2. **Plan for your mental road trips!** What do most people take with them on road trips? Some food, a phone with a mapping feature, some games, and usually emergency supplies, yeah? Emergency supplies are taken in case something goes wrong. Your brain likes to have supplies, too, in case there are future challenges. When you ask a what-if question, your brain is trying to plan ahead for future challenges to make sure you have the "supplies," or a plan. Sometimes your brain just needs a little help creating the plan. It's time to kick-start the planning process by writing down your what-if question and following up with if-then plans.

Example:

What if I raise my hand and say the wrong answer and everyone laughs?

IF I raise my hand and get the wrong answer and everyone laughs,

THEN I'll laugh along with them and remember that making mistakes helps my brain grow and we all make mistakes.

Write out your what-if questions and make some IF-THEN plans!

MENTAL
Road Trips

What if _____
_____?

IF _____

_____,

THEN _____

_____.

What if _____
_____?

IF _____

_____,

THEN _____

_____.

What if _____
_____?

IF _____

_____,

THEN _____

_____.

3. Calculate risk! When you worry, the part of your brain that figures out how risky something is might get a little foggy. That's why if you worry about going on an airplane and someone tells you that flying is less dangerous than driving, you might still worry. The exercise on the next page will help that tool in your brain wake up again so that you can be sure you're not over-worrying.

- Humans spend half their time thinking about the past and the future. This can cause a form of worry that we call What-iffing.

- You can work on What-iffing by being proactive with your thoughts: by being realistic, by making if-then plans, and by assessing risk.

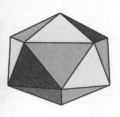

Calculate the Risk

What's the WORST thing that can happen?

What's the BEST thing that can happen?

What's the most LIKELY thing that can happen?

CHAPTER 6
CAMOUFLAGED

Carlos was halfway through his first day at a new school. He walked into the cafeteria, but it might as well have been a jungle. The lunch tables were filled with creatures of all kinds: athletes, drama kids, gamers. . . . At least, that's how it felt. Either way, he was the unknown species. His heart was thumping so loud, he was sure everyone could hear it. He looked around and saw someone smiling. For a split second he thought about smiling back, but what if the smile wasn't for him? Better to play it safe and look away.

He felt so awkward, like he didn't even belong in his own skin. Everyone else must have seen how horribly out of place he felt. He glanced around again, looking for a place to sit. He thought he might have a little bit in common with some of the kids, but what if he didn't? Where did he fit?

"Just take a deep breath," his mom had said that morning.

"Try to relax. You'll be fine," his dad had said as Carlos had walked out the door.

Those things never work, *Carlos thought.*

Finally, someone tapped him on the shoulder. "Hey, you board?"

Board? What? Carlos was confused until he realized he'd been carrying around his brother's hand-me-down backpack, which was covered in skateboarding patches. But, unlike his brother, Carlos had never been on a skateboard. He paused, then finally said, "Uh, yeah, I board. Like, all the time."

The boy pointed to an empty seat next to him and his friends. Carlos sat, relieved not to be eating alone. But instead of enjoying the conversation, he was super nervous that one of the other kids was going to ask a question about something he knew nothing about, and his lie would be revealed.

If you feel like you don't know where you fit in some of the time, or even most of the time, you're not alone. It hurts. We all want to be accepted. We all want to be invited to hang with friends without having to fight our way into a group. We all worry that we don't truly belong. And sometimes we worry so

much, we feel so strongly that we *should* fit in, that we abandon our superpower of being **Original** and pretend to be someone we're not. We Camouflage our true selves, even if it doesn't feel good.

Camouflaging means you cover up your true feelings and behaviors and transform into someone you *think* you need to be in order to fit into a situation, or to make others happy.

You might do things like:

- Pretend to enjoy hobbies or sports you've never tried.
- Talk about music you know nothing about.
- Change your behavior, perhaps in negative ways.
- Act differently on social media than you do in real life.
- Dress in clothes that make you uncomfortable.
- Act unkindly to others, to "boost" yourself.
- Hide things that *you* like in case others think those things aren't cool.

Or you may go into true Camouflage mode and do whatever it takes to *not* be noticed.

Scientists have learned that when a person feels left out, that feeling can activate the same parts of the brain that are activated when we feel physical pain. So rejection can *literally* hurt. It's awful. It's no wonder we try our best to fit in somewhere—anywhere. But the problem is that when we Camouflage, we're hurting ourselves; we're not being our **Original** and true selves.

Social Anxiety

Social anxiety, or intense fear of social situations, is fueled by worrying about what other people think of you. You might worry so much that you even start to avoid certain people or activities. Check out the list below—and circle anything that makes you feel worried.

Answering questions in class or in public

Going to parties or social activities

Going into a room where people are already sitting

Getting teased or laughed at

Performing in public

Inviting friends to do something

Giving speeches

Joining a conversation

Talking to adults

Making eye contact

Being the center of attention

Asking a teacher for help

Feeling caught between friends

Meeting new people

Starting conversations with someone you like

If you circled any of those activities, then you're in good company . . . with 7.5 billion other people! That's right. At some point, every single human has felt uncomfortable or anxious in a social situation. You might feel like you're going through this on your own, and other kids you know have socially perfect lives. That just isn't the case. You are not alone. You are amazing. You are superpowered. You are simply in something we call the worry runaround, and we're going to help get you out.

The Worry Runaround

The worry runaround is a cycle—and when you're stuck in it, you feel worse and worse with every go-around. Here's how it works: Worry messages show up. Maybe they're about your social life. Whatever the worry, those messages affect your thoughts, your feelings, and your actions—or what you think, feel, and do.

Think: The worry messages pass through your mind. Examples might be *I worry too much* or *She really doesn't like me* or *I sound like I don't know what I'm talking about* or *This is why nobody likes me.*

Feel: The way we think about the worry affects what we feel in our bodies. In this case, we're worried about our worry. The result is a battle in our bodies—we might feel feverish, nausea, racing thoughts, sweaty hands, dizziness, and exhaustion.

Do: Your thoughts and feelings lead to what you do. Maybe you run away. If you're worried about going to a party, maybe you pretend to be sick to avoid it. It's these actions that can lead you right back into the runaround, increasing your worry and starting the cycle over again.

At the beginning of this chapter, we met Carlos, who was in the worry runaround. Here's what it looked like.

WORRY MESSAGES

You're having lunch at a new school!

THINK

"Everyone must notice I'm SO awkward."

"Wait, did that girl just smile? There's no way it was at me."

"No one is ever going to ask me to sit with them."

FEEL

Heart racing
Palms sweating
Dry throat

DO

Avoid eye contact.
Lie about skateboarding.
Eat with the first kid who speaks to me.

To help him (and you!), we're going to work on the "Think" part of the worry runaround. It's been a while since we dropped some hard truth, so here we go: many of your thoughts aren't true. And when you're worried, thoughts can be even more untrue. Really!

You can have thousands of thoughts every day, and *a lot* of those thoughts are exaggerated, unrealistic, twisted, distorted, and just flat-out wrong. If our thoughts were playing a game of darts, they'd miss the bull's-eye most of the time. If our thoughts were candy, they'd be taffy you could stretch and twist. If our thoughts were part of a carnival, they'd be the fun-house mirror. What we're trying to say is that thoughts aren't always what they seem; a lot of times they contain errors or mistakes.

At the beginning of the chapter, Carlos saw someone smiling at him but thought he was being ignored. This was a thinking mistake. We call these thinking mistakes ThoughtHoles. When it comes to social situations, there are five common ThoughtHoles we fall into. HOLES is an acronym for Hunchifying, Overlooking, Lightifying, Extremifying, and Supersizing.

DID YOU KNOW?

Every second, you can take in eleven million pieces of information through your senses and subconscious mind. Amazing! However, you can only pay attention to between seven and forty bits at a time. From eleven million to just seven? Your brain needs to filter out information so you don't go into sensory overload!

This means that if you're at a baseball game, your senses might take in nine players on the field, three loaded bases and a batter, packed dugouts and bullpens, thousands of fans, grass and dirt, banners and advertisements, a hundred stats on the scoreboard, cheers, chants, and music, smells of peanuts and hot dogs and popcorn, the temperature, the time, bats and balls, and thousands of other things. BUT you can't possibly pay conscious attention to everything! Maybe you only watch the runner at first base and focus on the taste of your lemonade. Paying attention to only a few things in your surroundings is a mental shortcut. Shortcuts help us make sense of the world, but because we're judging situations based on just a little bit of information, we make mistakes.

HUNCHIFYING

Having a hunch or guessing at
what another person is thinking
or how a situation will turn out

OVERLOOKING

Looking past or ignoring the positive or
good stuff in a situation and focusing
mostly on negative or bad stuff

LIGHTIFYING

Feeling like there is a spotlight
turned on you and everyone is
judging you in a negative way

EXTREMIFYING

Viewing a situation in extremes,
using terms like "always"
or "never" or "the worst"

SUPERSIZING

Making a small challenge
much bigger than it is,
or exaggerating

Carlos was stressed about fitting in at his new school. He couldn't figure out who to sit with and was starting to worry. Carlos's thoughts were full of errors. Look at these scenes and see if you can figure out which ThoughtHole Carlos was in. Write in your answers in the blank lines that follow the scenes.

_____

_____

_____

_____

Answer: Carlos was Hunchifying, or guessing what the other person was thinking. Carlos guessed that the kid who asked him about skateboarding wouldn't like Carlos if he didn't skateboard.

Answer: Carlos was Supersizing, or exaggerating his fears, when he thought the lunchroom was like a jungle.

_____

_____

_____

_____

Answer: Carlos was Extremifying, or viewing the situation in extremes, when he thought he might "never" fit in with his new classmates.

93

_____

_____

_____

_____

Answer: Carlos was Overlooking, or ignoring the good stuff, when he didn't believe someone could actually be smiling at him.

Now that you know all about the worry runaround and ThoughtHoles, it's time to learn how they show up in your life.

Your Worry Runaround!

When you get a worry message, it affects what you think, feel, and do. Think about a social situation or any situation that has caused you worry, and fill out your runaround. Don't forget to draw yourself in the middle!

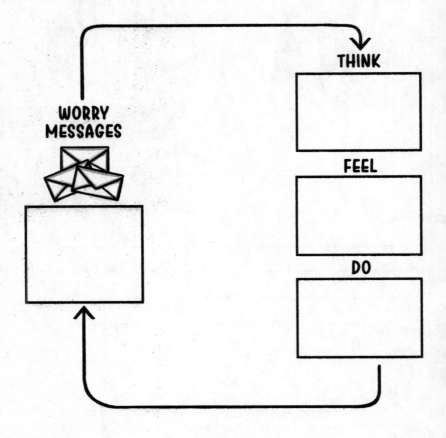

Fix the HOLES!

When you're in a ThoughtHole, you aren't thinking accurately. To fix the HOLES, we're going to use something developed by Renee's company, GoZen!, called the 5Cs process. In this process you will:

1. Catch your worried thought.
2. Check to see if you're in a ThoughtHole.
3. Collect evidence that goes against your thought.
4. Challenge your thought by debating yourself.
5. Change your thought to something more accurate.

The following example walks you through the 5Cs, and then you can try the process on your own!

1. CATCH *START
YOUR THOUGHT

Fill in a worried thought:

Everyone always stares at me when I walk into school and thinks my clothes are weird.

2.
CHECK
FOR HOLES

Extremifying—
I used the word "always."

Lightifying—
I think everyone is paying attention and judging me.

☐ **HUNCHIFYING**
Guessing at what another person is thinking or how a situation will turn out

☐ **OVERLOOKING**
Looking past or ignoring the positive or good stuff in a situation and focusing mostly on negative or bad stuff

☒ **LIGHTIFYING**
Feeling like there is a spotlight turned on you and everyone is judging you in a negative way

☒ **EXTREMIFYING**
Viewing a situation in extremes, using terms like "always" or "never" or "the worst"

☐ **SUPERSIZING**
Making a small challenge much bigger than it is, or exaggerating

Laddering!

In most worry runarounds, the "Do" section is filled out with words like the following: "ran away," "ignored," "pretended like it didn't exist," etc. In other words, we end up *avoiding* the situation or person that makes us worry. We've read lots of scientific research on the topic of avoidance, and here it is in a nutshell: avoiding what you worry about eventually makes your anxiety worse.

What we need is a plan to *avoid avoiding*. Yes, that's a double negative, which we're sure you know makes a positive, and in this case "positive" means exposure. Showing up, little by little, to the person or situation that you worry about will eventually end your worry. We like to call this gradual approach laddering. Try it!

Think about a situation or person that you avoid and that you would love to stop avoiding. Think about your goal in this situation. Here's an example: *I want to start a conversation with Jeremy.*

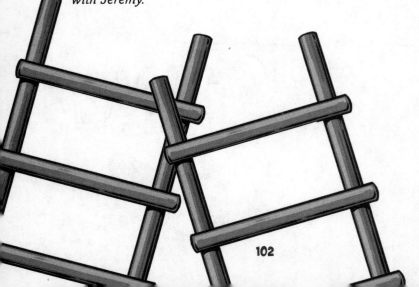

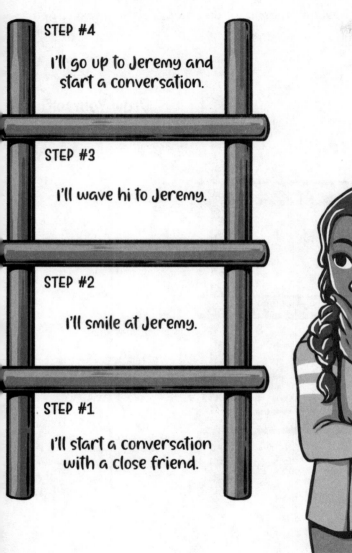

STEP #4

I'll go up to Jeremy and start a conversation.

STEP #3

I'll wave hi to Jeremy.

STEP #2

I'll smile at Jeremy.

STEP #1

I'll start a conversation with a close friend.

Your ladder can be taller or shorter. You do each step on the ladder several times, until that step feels too easy. Then you move up to the next step.

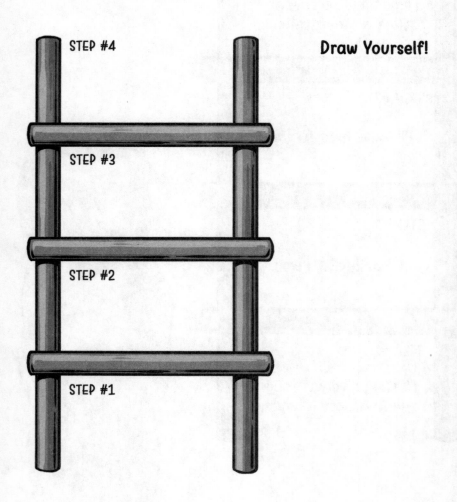

STEP #4

Draw Yourself!

STEP #3

STEP #2

STEP #1

KEY TAKEAWAYS

- The pain of rejection activates similar parts of the brain as physical pain, so it's not a surprise that you try to change yourself to avoid rejection and fit into social situations. This is Camouflaging.

- The worry runaround shows how situations that make you worry lead to worried thoughts, feelings, and actions.

- Your thoughts can be inaccurate or have mistakes that we call ThoughtHoles. You can challenge those ThoughtHoles with the 5Cs process.

CHAPTER 7
COCOONED

I'm not going 2 make it 2 piano recital tomorrow. Sry.

Oh no! What happened? You've been practicing for months! Tomorrow is the big day!

Got super sick. Sry 2 let u down.

Sick? You just left practice two hours ago. What happened? I know you were nervous, but...

I'm not nervous. Who said I was nervous? Just don't feel good. That's why I kept messing up today.

Do you want to wait and see if you feel better tomorrow?

Nope. Too sick.

It's okay to make mistakes, you know. I thought you had a good practice. You don't have to be perfect.

Hello?

What does being a perfectionist mean to you? Does it mean having high standards? Does it mean setting lofty goals? Is it about performance? Looks? Never resting until something is right?

Everyone has their own understanding of perfectionism. But here's a secret: In our experience, perfectionism is one of the most misunderstood concepts around! That's right. For a lot of kids (and even adults), being a perfectionist isn't about getting better at something. It's about *already* being the best at something. As you know, most of us don't start out being perfect at anything. In fact, we usually start out being pretty bad, and then with effort and practice, we get better. But when you're a perfectionist, you don't want anyone to see those stages of learning. You want to hide the work, the flaws, the practice, the trial and error. You want to pretend like none of those things are necessary. You want to start out, well, perfect.

So here's the thing: perfectionism is a problem not because it's about doing everything right but because it's often about **doing nothing at all.** Perfectionism is about avoidance. Avoiding challenges. Avoiding practice and effort. Avoiding risks. Avoiding people who might be more skilled than us. Avoiding anything whatsoever that might bring us within reach of a mistake or a failure. So while most people believe that perfectionism is about striving to be something exceptional, it's really about the opposite. And of course, we're here to tell you what you can do about it.

But before we do, check out this quick quiz. And don't worry about your answers. This quiz (well, this whole book, actually) was written by a couple of recovering perfectionists!

Do you feel like you have to be the best at everything you do?	Yes or No
Are you embarrassed by mistakes?	Yes or No
Are you worried about disappointing friends, parents, or teachers?	Yes or No
Do you avoid projects or performances because you're afraid you won't be good at them?	Yes or No
When you do homework or a project, do you go over it again and again because you need it to be perfect?	Yes or No
Do you fear getting feedback from your family or friends?	Yes or No
Do you spend a long time making decisions because you are afraid to make the wrong one?	Yes or No
Do you like to plan things many months in advance because you are worried that if you don't, something will go wrong?	Yes or No
Do you make excuses (e.g., "I'm not feeling great") before you have to perform or take a test?	Yes or No
Do you think over and over about the mistakes you've made?	Yes or No

There have been times in our own lives when we've circled YES to everything on that list! Don't be alarmed if you did the same thing. It just means that you're *human,* and you may be a little bit of a perfectionist. The first step in overcoming those unhealthy habits is awareness of what's going on.

Perfectionism is about hiding our imperfections and not taking risks, because we feel vulnerable. When we feel vulnerable to failure, we spin protective Cocoons around ourselves, to shield us from the threat of any error. Most perfectionists we know have lost their superpowers and end up Cocooned.

COCOONED

7 WAYS PERFECTIONISM GOES WRONG

1 never "GOOD ENOUGH"-ness

2 needing to be pleasing

3 FEARING FLUBS

Cocoons are not comfortable places to live. Sure, being Cocooned may keep you from making mistakes, but it also keeps you from doing—well, anything! Cocoons don't make you work harder. They don't make you gritty and determined. *And* Cocoons don't allow anyone to see the real you. So, what can you do to get out of your Cocoon?

We can learn from others going through the same thing. As you know, we've met a lot of kids and heard a lot of stories. Here are seven different ways that Cocoons and perfectionism have gotten in the way of these kids' superpowers, as well as the strategies they used (and you can, too!) to break through the Cocoon.

Nadya's Never-Good-Enoughness

When Nadya looked in the mirror, she always found something wrong. Her hair was straight, but she wanted it curly. When she curled it, it kind of looked flat and blah. She hated all of her clothes, but when she got new ones, she hated the way they fit. And the Never-Good-Enoughness didn't stop with her appearance. She once showed us an exam she had studied very hard for. She'd gotten a 96, but instead of being thrilled, all she talked about was how she'd fallen short of 100. Her posts didn't get "enough" likes. She didn't have "enough" friends. She didn't get "enough" done. Nadya never felt like enough.

SOLUTION: Let's do a quick thought experiment. What if a teacher told you that you'd gotten 39 points? There's no other information besides that number. You don't know if it's 39 points in a game or on a test, or how you earned them. Do you think 39 points is good? Hard to know, right? Without comparing this number to someone else's points, or to the highest possible points, or to the class average, "good" and "bad" just don't make sense. Nadya learned that her feeling not good enough was based on a belief that she held involving comparison. Nadya compared her 96 on a test to the highest possible 100 and decided that 96 wasn't "good enough." Here are the tools Nadya used to move past this feeling:

What's Under the Duck?

When you see someone doing something that you think is "better" than you (getting a higher grade, playing a better sports position, having or doing a better anything), it's a lot like seeing a duck gliding successfully across water. The duck makes it look easy from the surface, but you don't see what's under the duck: legs kicking furiously in the water. When you feel like success comes easier to someone else, make sure you look under the duck! Write in some more words above the water (the accomplishments of others that you see) and below in the water (the effort and hard work that you don't necessarily see).

Flip the Switch

Go ahead and compare yourself to others; it happens all the time, and we're not going to tell you not to do it. But when you do compare yourself to someone else, flip the switch. Flip from feeling envy to feeling inspired. Someone have better style than you? What can you learn from them? Someone play better hoops than you? What effort are they making that can inspire you? How do you go from envious to inspired? Visualize this as a switch that you flip inside yourself.

Fill in this sentence to help flip your switch:

I'm inspired by _____

and how they _____

This is the action I'm inspired to take:

_____

_____

Philippe's Need to Please

Everyone loved Philippe as soon as they met him. He was so friendly and polite! People always seemed to find common ground with him. It seemed like he would do or say anything to make people happy. It turns out that was exactly his plan. Philippe was so worried about conflict, so worried about not being perfect in the eyes of others, that he completely sacrificed himself. He NEVER disagreed with anyone. He was on the gymnastics team because he was afraid to tell his mom he no longer wanted to be. He always agreed to help people, even when it left him with no time for himself. Philippe's Cocoon protected him from the potentially negative opinions of others, but made him feel miserable and incomplete most of the time.

SOLUTION: Philippe realized he was giving away all his *life juice*. Your life juice comes from the essential things you need to take in or do every day to help you feel your best. You already know some of the ingredients: food and sleep. But the other things are just as essential: saying no when you don't want to do something, protecting your time, and living in sync with your values. If you're not doing any of these things because you're trying to please other people, then your juice gets used up and you start to worry. Philippe started to fill up his juice in different areas. Where do you need to fill up your juice? What would you add to your self-care? Draw your essentials in the image.

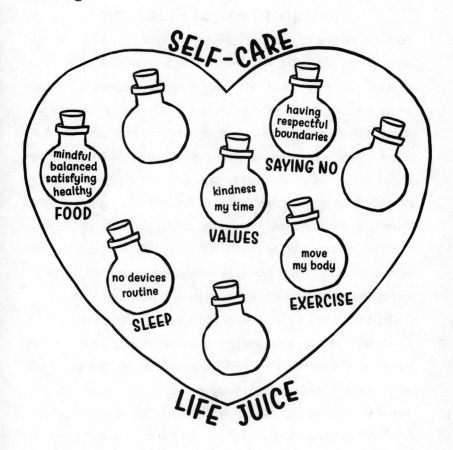

Joslyn's Fear of Flubbing

Joslyn was one of the hardest-working kids in school, but her teacher and the other kids around her probably wouldn't have guessed. She never raised her hand in class, even when she was pretty sure she knew the answer. She never wanted her artwork hung up in the classroom, even though she was incredibly creative. She never played kickball at recess, even though she loved practicing at home. See, Joslyn was so afraid of saying the wrong thing, being judged, or just plain failing to be perfect that she often did nothing at all. And when she did put herself out there and make a mistake, she struggled to forgive herself and she apologized to everyone, treating herself like she'd committed some horrible crime. For the people who loved her, it was hard to watch.

SOLUTION: Joslyn learned to be a YETi! We don't mean she turned into an abominable snowman. She just learned the power of the word "YET"! She learned that no one starts off as an expert in anything. Imagine if everyone came into the world already an expert in everything. . . . What would that be like? We might as well be robots! As humans, we all start off imperfect and get better with practice and effort. This process can be really rewarding! You didn't come into the world walking or talking, but you tried and failed and then tried again until you finally learned to do those things. The same thing goes with *anything* you're trying to learn. If you start something and you're not good at it, try to use this one powerful word: "YET." Change sentences like "I'm not good at this" to "I'm not good at this . . . YET." Fill in the exercise below:

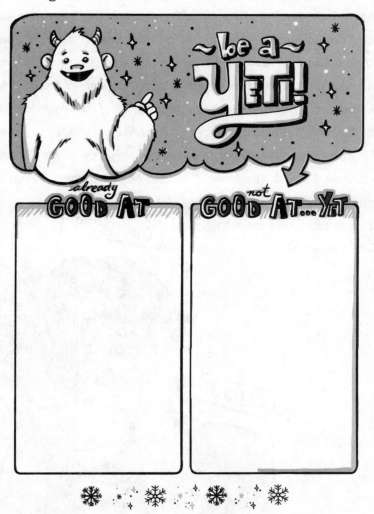

Clayton's Supersized Organizing

Clayton's parents noticed he was stressed out about school. He was constantly making to-do lists, was keeping pages of detailed notes, had the whole year scheduled on a calendar, and organized his homework and desk flawlessly. And if anything was ever out of place or changed, he'd get super upset. To help him take a break and relax, his parents planned a surprise trip to Florida for their family. While the trip wasn't a bad idea, the surprise might have been a mistake. It would be an understatement to say that Clayton was anxious when he learned they were getting on a plane the next day. What if he forgot to pack something? What if he missed something important at school? What if they overslept for the flight? What would their schedule be like once they got there? Clayton wanted everything to always go perfectly, so his Cocoon was spun from plans, alarms, lists, and endless details. He had a really hard time with anything spontaneous, even something as fun as vacation.

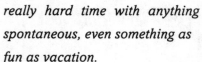

SOLUTION: Clayton realized that when anything unexpected happened, he was totally thrown off track from his goals, and it made him worry *a lot*. That is, until he learned to WOOP! Like Clayton, most goal setters only focus on the end or the actual goal. While that seems to make sense, the number one reason why people don't reach a goal is because they face an obstacle that throws them off course. There's a goal-setting method created by some rad scientists that focuses both on the goal itself and creating plans to overcome possible obstacles. It's also kinda fun to say: WOOP! This method helps keep you on track even if obstacles arise, because you already have a plan in place for dealing with any problems. You can use the diagram on the following page to set your next goal using the WOOP method, which stands for "Wish, Outcome, Obstacle, Plan."

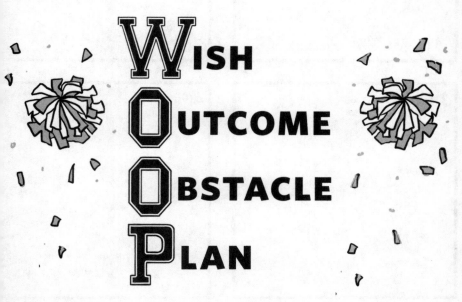

WISH

OUTCOME

OBSTACLE

PLAN

WOOP, THERE IT IS!

Try setting your next goal using the WOOP method (Wish, Outcome, Obstacle, Plan) by writing or drawing in the boxes below.

1. Wish

ex: "I want to get a B or higher on my history test."

2. Outcome

ex: "I'll feel really good about it."

3. Obstacle

ex: "I have a hard time studying. I procrastinate a lot."

4. Plan

ex: "If I procrastinate when I'm supposed to study, then I'll call my friend to come study with me."

Fynn the Perfectionism Police

It's one thing to Cocoon yourself, to try to protect yourself from mistakes at all costs. But Fynn took it to the next level. He spun his Cocoon around everyone close to him as well. He was constantly correcting people and telling them how to do things "better." He often complained about the other kids on his soccer team and made comments about their plays. Food at restaurants was never cooked the right way, and he liked to tell the waitstaff about it. While Fynn was loved by friends and family, he wasn't always easy to be around. He needed everyone to know that his standards were high. Luckily, he began to recognize his worry, his Cocoon, and his unfortunate need to share his perfectionism with others.

That's not good enough!

SOLUTION: Fynn figured it was time to let go of things that were out of his control. This one is much easier said than done, but the first step is pretty simple: figure out what's in your control. The things in your control are the things you're able to change a little bit or a lot with your own actions. After figuring those things out, focus your attention on them. Start to make changes where you want to make them. When you do this, you'll naturally spend less time worrying about the things out of your control.

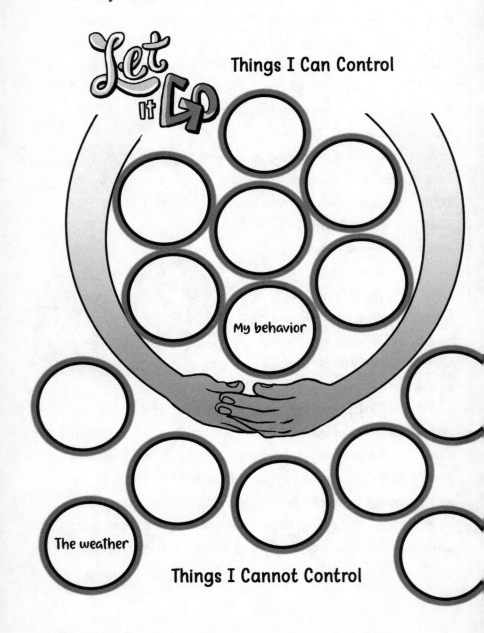

Let it Go

Things I Can Control

My behavior

The weather

Things I Cannot Control

I'll just do it later....

Lydia Living in Procrasti-Nation

Lydia had been labeled by people in all kinds of unkind ways. She'd been referred to as disorganized, a poor planner, slow, unmotivated, and just plain lazy. Sure, she put lots of things off until the last minute, and she was often late for things, but she didn't think that made her lazy. And she was right! The reason Lydia procrastinated was because she, too, was Cocooned. She would worry so much about making mistakes on projects, on homework, or socially that she delayed taking care of her responsibilities. Lydia lived in procrasti-nation.

SOLUTION: Lydia realized that her goals felt too big. She was so overwhelmed by her goals that she would give up before she even started. This led to procrastination. So, instead of setting big, worry-making goals, Lydia learned to make itty-bitty goals. This is just like when marathon runners break up the big 26.2-mile goal into many shorter distances, like setting a target of hitting 5 miles, or even just 2 miles.

We want you to break your big goals into smaller goals. In fact, make them so small that the goal might even seem silly. The point is that you've made them so itty-bitty that it's impossible to *not* do them—it's impossible to fail! This might

ITTY-BITTY GOALS

BIG GOAL: _____

Itty-Bitty
Goal

mean that your first goal could be to "write one sentence" or "do one jumping jack" or "open your book." It doesn't matter. Taking the first step to complete a goal is the only way to get it done! Science shows us that taking action is twice as effective as changing your thinking. So don't worry if you don't feel like doing something, and do it anyway!

Nobody here likes you.

Marsheila's Inner Monster

People of all ages often talk about voices in their heads—inner thoughts, the sound of one's own worry. In Marsheila's case, she didn't just have inner thoughts. She had an inner monster. Her thoughts were not kind to her: You're not good enough to be here! Nobody here likes you. If you don't study more, you're going to fail for sure. You'll never be as good as Claudia. *Marsheila's thoughts eventually got the best of her, and she stopped trying. She stopped putting herself out into the world. She Cocooned.*

SOLUTION: Marsheila knew deep inside that she would never, ever speak to her friends the way she spoke to herself inside her head. We call the unkind voice she experienced the "inner monster." The inner monster not only can make you feel terrible, but as science has shown us, it also can make it harder for you to reach your goals. Here's how Marsheila learned to change that voice: she started writing letters to herself as though she were her own best friend. Write a short note to yourself below in the voice of your best friend. It can be on any topic you want; just remember that the person writing it cares about you a lot.

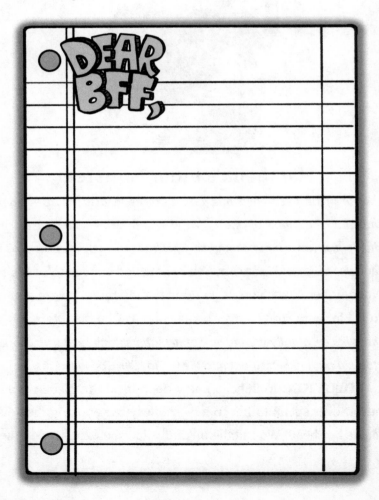

If I Don't Need to Be Perfect, Then What?

For some, perfectionism will always mean hard work, dedication, high standards, and trying your hardest, and that's great! Those are all amazing qualities! And we'd love for you to keep all the useful parts of perfectionism while shedding everything that causes pain. We'd love for you to lose the worry Cocoon so that you can rediscover your superpower of being **Whole**!

- Perfectionism isn't about always getting things right; it's about fearing failure and avoiding situations in which you might make a mistake.

- When you try to appear perfect, eventually you stop engaging with your own life. You are Cocooned.

- When you're Cocooned, you're trying to protect yourself from mistakes, but you also prevent yourself from taking risks, growing, and experiencing life.

2tired already. only 6am. if you ask me life's feeling like such a trap. all this so i can be successful??? doesn't feel worth it. going back to bed #toomuchtodo

CHAPTER 8
FRIED

So much to do all the time. But why? "Why?" is a good question to ask. It's one of the first we ever learn, and it's one we should never stop asking. Why do we have so much to do? Why do we do math homework? Why do I practice an instrument? Why do I need to clean my room? These are all good questions, and we're guessing that if we asked you these things, you'd have some pretty simple answers ready: "Because I need to get good grades." "Because I need a scholarship for college." "Because I need a good job." "Because I need my own house someday." So many of the kids we've spoken to—kids of all different ages—have given us the same answers over the years that we're starting to think everyone is following some secret map with those very destinations on it—good grades, college, good job, owning a house. It's as if we all need to follow a specific route or we'll get lost on the way to leading a good life. In fact, if such a map existed, that wouldn't be a bad name for it—the Good-Life Map.

The map would be BIG and include lots of stops that take

years to reach. What an exhausting trip. No wonder so many of you come to us Fried! On the map, there's just one narrow road that leads to just one destination that we all want to reach—happiness. Does the path look familiar? If you follow the road and get good grades, join extracurricular activities, get into a good college, eventually get married and have kids, then you'll FINALLY reach your goal of HAPPINESS!

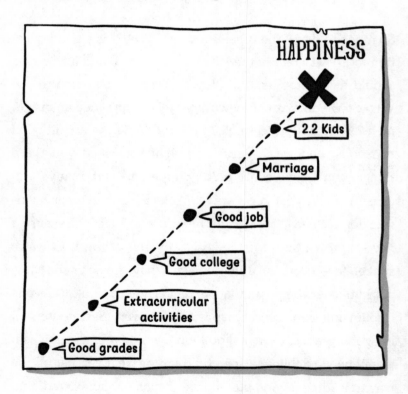

Most of us have a map like this in our lives. It includes all the goals, big and small, that we believe will lead to happiness.

Maybe yours looks slightly different. Draw your own Good-Life map here:

Of course, there are some major problems with these maps. First, the moment you veer off the narrow road—even slightly—you fall into a sea of worry, anxiety, and fear.

Second, and even more problematic, the destination—happiness—doesn't actually exist. How's that for a truth bomb?

We know what you're thinking: *Of course happiness exists!* You're right. Of course it exists. We've felt it, and it's awesome.

It just doesn't exist in the way that most people think it does. But we'll come back to that in a sec. Let's finish talking about the issues with the map.

The third problem with the map is that the road itself isn't safe. It's full of hazards. When you follow this road to happiness and hit all the problems on the way, your superpower of being **Energized** (being full of zest for life and a passion for learning) gets zapped and you end up Fried (exhausted, depleted, and constantly worried).

Let's take a closer look so we can see all the places along the road that cause problems and lead you right to being Fried!

Bad Road Signs: Shoulding

You start taking all the "shoulds" you've heard in your life, and you start repeating them in your mind. *I* should *get good grades,* and *I* should *work harder,* and *I* should *be in a lot of activities,* and *I* should *be more social.*

Broken Guardrails: No Room for Mistakes

You have no room for error. The road to happiness is very narrow. The moment you do go off the road (for example, getting a bad grade), you fall into the sea of worry.

False Advertising:
Incorrect Motivation

The road isn't easy to drive, but to keep you moving along, sometimes teachers, parents, and other adults dangle rewards and praise or even ground and punish you to help motivate you. All this may be done out of love, but eventually those things aren't motivating.

Tailgating:
Following Others Too Closely

Sometimes you do reach some of your goals, but you don't have time to celebrate because you see everyone else around you zipping to accomplish the next thing. You can't enjoy the journey, stop and smell the roses, feel grateful, or any of that stuff because you're busy moving on.

False Identity:
Bumper Stickers

Your identity is tied to things you've achieved. You forget who you really are and become one with your test scores, trophies, and achievements. These successes are temporary and something to take pride in, but they don't define your identity.

Find the Obstacles!

At the beginning of this chapter, you saw a social media post from one of our friends who's feeling Fried. We'd like to tell you a little more about him, and we'd like you to identify some of the stops on his Good-Life Map. Do you think you can also tell us which obstacles he's finding on the road that are leading to him feeling Fried?

Franklin did it all. Sports, orchestra, tutoring other kids in the math lab. Super busy, all the time. He was the youngest of four children, and he always had these awesome role models in front of him. His oldest sister was the valedictorian at their school and ended up with a scholarship to a great university. His older brother was the star basketball player on the team and had a million friends. His other sister was a cello prodigy. Franklin was an honor roll student, was great at jujitsu (which made him happier than anything else he did), and was a decent violin player. But somehow it just never felt like enough. He needed to do more. He pushed himself into some harder classes, he signed up for basketball, and he woke up at four a.m. to practice violin in the basement every day. The classes stressed him out, he found basketball boring, and he was exhausted all the time, but the harder classes helped his GPA, he made more friends playing hoops, and he moved up a chair in the orchestra.

Franklin's aunt and uncle had both gone to college, and they lived in a beautiful house. There was a home theater in the basement, a shower with two showerheads, and a yard big enough to get lost in. From the first time he visited them as a young kid, he knew that he wanted to live like that when he grew up. "If you want to get ahead," his aunt once said to him, "you should just try to work harder than the guy next to you." Simple enough, *Franklin thought. He never forgot those words. It's what motivated him. Those words, and that house.*

But by the time Franklin got to us, he had lost most of his energy and ambition. He was Fried, and it showed. His grades started to fall because he didn't feel like studying anymore. He was terrified that he wouldn't make the honor roll again. He quit jiujitsu, the one thing he loved, because he didn't have the energy after basketball. He lost a few close friends because he was so tired and crabby all the time. And he felt more and more anxious with every day that went by. His superpower of being Energized was missing.

1. Use the space below to draw Franklin's Good-Life Map.
2. Add in the obstacles Franklin faced on his road.

The Problem with Happiness

We want to be clear—we have nothing against happiness. Who doesn't want to feel happy? Feeling happy is amazing! We just think there are some HUGE misunderstandings and myths about what happiness really is. To help explain the problem with happiness, we think it might be time for some . . .

Myth Busting!

MYTH #1: Happiness is a destination. On the Good-Life Map, happiness looks like a place you reach after accomplishing a bunch of goals. That means, once you get to the destination of happiness, you should then *feel* happy forever. After all, you've reached the end of the road! But happiness is a FEELING, and feelings don't work that way. Have you ever felt *any* feeling forever? Exactly! Feelings come and go. So, never *feel bad* that you don't *feel good* every second of the day. Again, happiness isn't a place where you land and then feel happy all the time. **Reality: Happiness is a wonderful feeling that comes and goes throughout our lives.**

MYTH #2: Happiness comes from achieving goals. Many times after we reach a goal, we think we're supposed to feel happy. It's confusing, even disappointing, when sometimes you make a new friend, get a good grade, or win a trophy and you just don't feel happy, or you only feel happiness for a moment. Many of us have spent our lives expecting happiness from reaching a goal. Over time, it takes MORE achievements, MORE goals, MORE anything to make you feel happy, until, eventually, achievements don't make you feel anything at all. **Reality: Happiness can be experienced while you're working on your goals, not just when you reach them.**

MYTH #3: Happiness is the only feeling worth having. When you focus only on being happy, you start to think that all the other feelings aren't worth that much. Maybe you've even heard from loving adults that they just want you to be happy. Maybe when you've experienced big feelings like anger, people have tried to calm you down. All of this may have led you to believe that feelings like sadness, guilt, and anger are useless or even *bad* to feel. Remember way back in chapter 4 when we talked about worry having a purpose? Then you probably can guess the reality here. **Reality: All feelings have value and are okay to feel.**

Feeling:	Message from your feeling:	Action to take:
Sadness	"You're experiencing a loss."	Heal
Anger	"Someone has done something unfair to you or you're in an unfair situation."	Enforce boundaries
Disgust	"You should reject that."	Protect health
Guilt	"You have done something wrong or hurt someone else."	Reconnect
Worry	"You're in danger. You're being challenged."	Keep safe, motivate

Find Your Icky Guy!

If you've been following the original Good-Life Map from above, you probably feel similarly to how early explorers felt when following a map of a flat Earth . . . confused and worn-out. In other words, you're Fried. Fried from your list of things to do. Fried from trying to reach lots of goals, including doing well in your schoolwork, finishing homework, sitting through classes, and making friends. Fried from trying to be less worried and happier all the time. Fried from feeling pressure from everything or everyone around you. We're going to help.

When humans realized that Earth is round, maps were redrawn. The time has come to **redraw your map.** Before you draw your new and improved map, here are some pointers:

Tip 1: Make sure your map has no destination. Yes, we know, this is going to feel totally bizarre, but life is not only about the end result. It's about the journey, including the ups, downs, and all-arounds along the way. Your new map isn't going to have a beginning or an end!

Tip 2: Forget the straight line. Who do you know who sets and reaches all their goals on the first try? No one! In fact, no one in the history of humankind has done that. Everyone takes detours, makes mistakes, takes breaks, gets confused, faces obstacles, thinks about things, and does all sorts of other stuff along the way. Life is not a straight line—it's super curvy.

Tip 3: Take a tip from the Okinawans. The citizens of Okinawa, Japan, live seven years longer than Americans on average. More people live to be centenarians, or one hundred years old or older, in Okinawa than anywhere else in the world! Heart disease, strokes, and cancer rates are low. Researchers were so intrigued by Okinawans, they studied what contributed to their long and healthy lives.

Here are some of the things they found: Okinawans eat until they are 80 percent full, they enter into friend groups as babies and grow old together, and they never retire. That's right, they don't even have a word for retirement! But they do have another awesome word: "Ikigai," pronounced "icky guy." This roughly translates to "the reason why you wake up in the morning." Ikigai is about figuring out your purpose and using it as a guide for what you do every day. It gives you driving force. Ikigai helps create a true path to a good life.

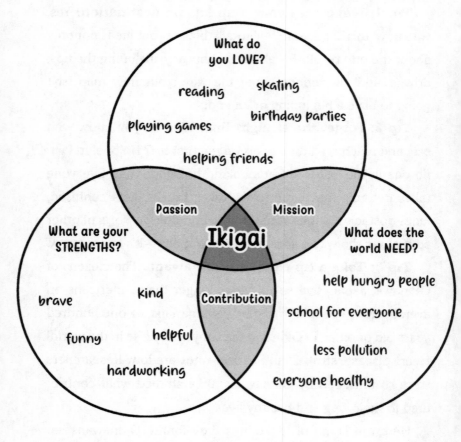

Time to draw your new map inspired by the concept of Ikigai. This is where what you love, your strengths, and what the world needs all intersect.

Fill in your Ikigai map.

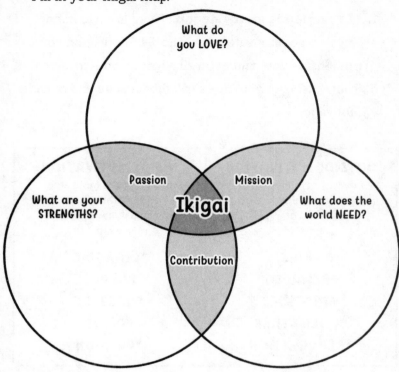

Take a picture of your filled-out map and keep it close by. Any time you feel like you need motivation, look at your Ikigai!

Now, we haven't forgotten that you've been feeling Fried. If you've been getting up in the morning without energy, if you've had trouble sleeping, if you don't feel motivated to learn or to do schoolwork, if you feel pressure to do well in all parts of your life but just don't feel like trying anymore, we understand that you're feeling Fried. You are not alone. We've created the next exercises just for you.

Try these exercises!

1. **Motivation is an inside job.** There are two main ways we get motivated: intrinsically (motivation comes from inside you) and extrinsically (motivation comes from outside of you). Let's call them inside and outside motivation.

OUTSIDE MOTIVATION	INSIDE MOTIVATION
means you're motivated to do something to earn an award or avoid a punishment.	means you're motivated to do something because you love it, have passion, or have curiosity.
*PRAISE	*LEARNING
*REWARDS	*PURPOSE
*TROPHIES	*MASTERY
*GOLD STARS	*PRIDE
*RECOGNITION	*PASSION

Test your know-how! Circle the motivation type after each example.

   a. Cleaning up your room because you like to stay organized: *Inside or Outside*
   b. Entering a contest to challenge yourself: *Inside or Outside*
   c. Writing a paper to get a good grade: *Inside or Outside*

d. Playing the viola to please your parents:
   Inside or Outside

e. Going to school to avoid punishment:
   Inside or Outside

f. Practicing soccer to win trophies:
   Inside or Outside

g. Playing video games because it's satisfying:
   Inside or Outside

Answers: (a) Inside (b) Inside (c) Outside (d) Outside (e) Outside (f) Outside (g) Inside

You've probably already guessed that, in thelong run, doing things because you're intrinsically motivated (motivated from the inside) helps you perform better, stay committed to the task for longer, and overcome obstacles. This doesn't mean that EVERYTHING you do will be or should be motivated from the inside, but there can be a balance. Draw a picture of yourself on the next page. Put inside your body the goals and tasks that you work on that are intrinsically motivated. Put outside of your body the goals and tasks that are extrinsically motivated.

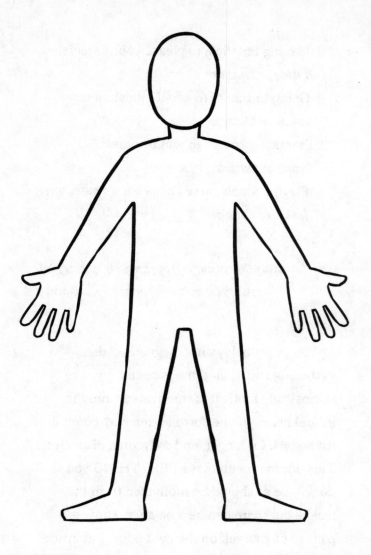

2. Find your flow. Have you ever been so absorbed in an activity—whether it's painting, running, or even playing a video game—that time just zips by? You might have been in a state that psychologists call "flow." Athletes

call it "being in the zone." Artists call it "rapture."
Flow. It's when you stop thinking and just *do*.

Flow happens when a challenge matches your skill
level, and you're working somewhere between boredom
and anxiety. The thing you're working on can't be too
challenging, or you'll feel anxious; it can't be too easy,
or you'll feel bored.

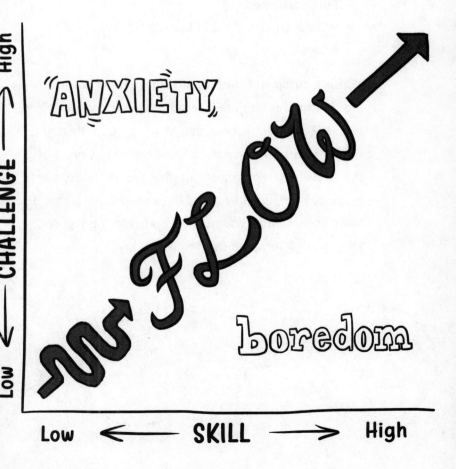

If you're feeling Fried, finding your flow can help. Figure out the activities that put you in flow!

- Which activity, hobby, interest, or passion do I work on where time just seems to pass by?
- What's an activity that's too easy for me and I get bored?
- What's an activity that's too hard for me and I get frustrated?
- What's an activity that has the perfect level of challenge for me?

3. **Make a sleep bubble!** Most kids we meet who are Fried are pretty tired. In other words, they aren't getting enough sleep. You might wake up in the night, wake up early, or have trouble falling asleep, or all of the above. We're not going to give you all the research on sleep here, because you can probably guess that it boils down to this: you need sleep to feel **Energized,** to grow, to learn, and even to worry less.

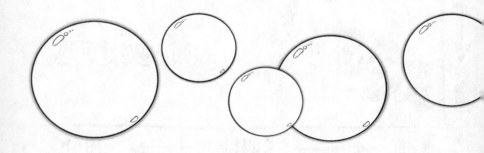

You probably already know you need sleep, but
how do you get it? One hour before you go to bed,
you're going to do all the things that help you get a
better night's sleep. This creates a protective shield
around you to give you the best shot at a good night's
rest. We call this protection the "sleep bubble." Turn
the page and draw your own:

a. In the blank bubble, draw your room and where you sleep.

b. Also in the bubble, write all the things that help you get a good night's sleep.

c. Outside the bubble, write all the things that don't help you get a good night's sleep.

d. Activate your sleep bubble one hour before sleeping each night.

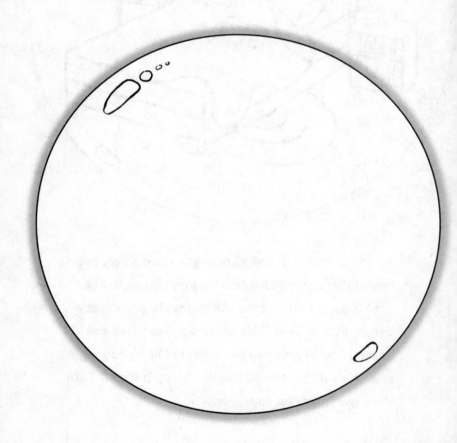

- While happiness is great, it's a temporary feeling, so setting it as a goal can leave you unsatisfied and feeling Fried.

- Figure out your Ikigai, or your reason for waking up each morning. This will always keep you motivated from within!

CHAPTER 9
ICED

Dear Mom and Dad,

I'm writing you a letter because sometimes talking makes me anxious. Thing is, I don't want to go to school anymore. It's not just because Micah moved away and I don't have too many people to hang out with. It's because every day when I'm there, I feel sick. Like yesterday, we played basketball in gym, and two kids were captains and got to pick the teams. I kept thinking, *what if I get picked last?* I stood there trying to act like I was fine while I was sweating and burning inside. Then, in science class, Mr. Hendricks made us switch lab partners. Now I'm working with someone I barely know! Talking to new people always makes me . . . I just can't. Next week, we have to give a speech in English class— like, a real speech!

I was sitting there in the cafeteria today thinking about all these things, and I felt like I couldn't breathe and I was dizzy and my heart hurt. I was so scared that I went to the nurse. I'm sure there were some kids whispering as I left. I was having a panic attack . . . again. That's when you picked me up. You asked me what happened, so this is it. Please, please, please, please don't make me go back. I don't want this to happen anymore. I'm not going back. Why is this happening to me? I hate feeling like this. Don't be mad.

~Cruz

When your superpower of being **Resilient** is zapped and you're Iced, it feels like the only way to stop worrying is to stop doing, well . . . everything. I mean, it kinda makes sense, right? But the hardest part is that most of the kids we meet who are Iced haven't just lost their **Resilience.** They've lost most, if not all, of their superpowers. They feel powerless, completely frozen, stuck. They don't feel like going to school. They don't want to do homework. They don't feel like hanging out with friends. In short, they don't want to do life.

Living life often means taking risks. But when you're Iced, risks feel like an invitation to the worry runaround. You don't want to do anything that might have the chance of sparking anxiety. Some of the young friends we know were hurting so badly from anxiety that they avoided leaving their house.

What's It Like to Be Iced?

- You want to avoid anything and everything that makes you worry.
- When you do avoid, you only feel temporary relief from the worry.
- You stop taking chances.
- Most of your other superpowers are zapped as well.

There's more. We've explained that being Iced makes you avoid people, places, and things that cause you worry. But avoiding *does not* actually help you feel better in the long run. In fact, research makes it really clear that AVOIDANCE just makes anxiety WORSE. Eventually, everything you avoid just builds up and leads to more anxiety, panic, anger, and sometimes hopelessness.

We get it. Humans are not good when our bodies feel uncomfortable. We get really freaked out and will do anything we can to make the discomfort stop. Here are a few other things we do that make panic worse. If you've been doing any of these things when you panic, you're not alone. It's time to try something that does work. We're going to give you the tools not just to defrost yourself and survive this experience, but to really start living your life in a way that's truly *superpowered*!

PANIC MADE WORSE

1

"Feel like" STATEMENTS

You <u>feel like</u> something more than panic or anxiety is happening to your body. **Sounds like:** *"I feel like something is terribly wrong with my body."*

2

DISTRACTION

You try to <u>distract</u> yourself from the discomfort. **Sounds like:** *"Something is wrong. I just need to watch TV, eat, and pretend it's not happening."*

3

FAULTY CONNECTIONS

You avoid people, places, or things that you <u>think</u> are <u>connected</u> to your panic. **Sounds like:** *"I had that panic attack because I went to the grocery store. I'm never going there again."*

Crushing Panic

WARNING: What you're going to read next
may sound a little scary, but we promise,
we're going to make it a lot less scary.

At the beginning of this chapter, Cruz said he was freaking out when he thought he might be picked last in gym class. He said sometimes he's burning inside, it's hard for him to breathe, and his heart hurts. Cruz was having panic attacks.

Here are some things other kids have said they feel when they have panic attacks:

"I could see my heart moving up and down through my clothes. I couldn't breathe. . . . I just wanted it to STOP. I started screaming."

"I knew something was really, really, really, really, really wrong."

"I was hot and sweaty all over. I felt like I needed to jump into a pool right then, but I was sitting in math class."

"I just wanted my mom. I knew she'd take me to a doctor, but I didn't even care, it hurt so bad."

"I felt like my skin was going to melt off. I was dizzy and totally confused."

What are panic attacks? Here's the definition from the Anxiety and Depression Association of America. "A panic attack is the abrupt onset of intense fear or discomfort that reaches a peak within minutes and includes at least four of the following symptoms":

Accelerated heart rate

Sweating

Trembling or shaking

Chest pain or discomfort

Sensations of shortness of breath

Feelings of choking

Nausea

Dizziness or light-headedness

Chills or hot flashes

Numbness or tingling

Feelings of unreality

Fear of losing control

Fear of dying

The big difference between a panic attack and other anxiety experiences is the INTENSITY of the feelings and the amount of TIME the feelings last. Panic attacks hit the body hard and usually are at their worst in the first ten minutes or so.

If you've had a panic attack, you know it feels horrible. Most people who have one will do anything to never feel that way again. You might immediately go Iced and start to avoid the people or places you were around when you had the attack, in the hopes of avoiding another. Yes, it makes sense that you try to avoid, but avoiding just doesn't work.

There is a better way.

The Huge Discovery

Before we give you one of the most powerful techniques to crush panic, we have to tell you about a huge discovery—and a huge misunderstanding. This gets a little science-y, but just stick with us for a second. Many years ago, scientists studied the way monkeys acted when they were near danger, like a snake slithering toward them. But certain monkeys wouldn't run away, or try to fight the snake, or even freeze in their tracks. Those monkeys just didn't seem afraid. It turns out that they had some damage to a tiny almond-shaped part of their brains called the amygdala (pronounced uh-MIG-duh-lah). People got really excited by this discovery, as well as by later studies featuring rats and humans that showed that their healthy amygdalas did activate when danger was near. So, putting two and two together, some scientists developed a common belief that the amygdala was a kind of fear center in the brain.

THE ASSUMPTION

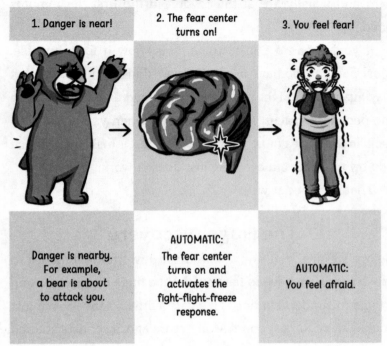

1. Danger is near!	2. The fear center turns on!	3. You feel fear!
Danger is nearby. For example, a bear is about to attack you.	AUTOMATIC: The fear center turns on and activates the fight-flight-freeze response.	AUTOMATIC: You feel afraid.

Here's what everyone got right: the amygdala automatically turns on when it senses a threat. The amygdala can automatically activate the fight, flight, or freeze response (remember the 3Fs from chapter 4?) to protect you. Again, all of that happens automatically, meaning you don't even have to think about it; you just react that way. It's not as if you tell your heart to race or your palms to sweat when you panic, right? It just happens. So, what was this huge misunderstanding? Just because your brain *automatically* senses danger and *automatically* turns on the 3Fs doesn't mean that you *automatically* feel fear.

Feeling afraid is *not* automatic. Feeling fear is more of a conscious process, or something you can think about. This is best explained if we imagine watching a scary movie.

THE MISSING STEP!!!

| 1. Danger is near! | 2. The ~~fear center~~ amygdala turns on! | 3. Choose your mindset. | 4. Choose your feeling. |

| Danger is nearby. For example, a bear is about to attack you. | AUTOMATIC: The amygdala turns on and activates the fight-flight-freeze response. | CHOICE: You think about what's happening to your body and judge whether or not you're really in danger. | CHOICE: You choose to feel afraid if you're really in danger. |

The Movie Theater Technique

Imagine this. You're sitting in a movie theater, safe and cozy in your chair. Popcorn. A cold drink. Suddenly something super scary happens in the movie! There's a scream, some spooky music, a loud THUD, and a crack of lightning! You gasp! Drop your popcorn! Maybe even hop out of your seat! You feel your heart racing, you're short of breath, and other panicky things are happening to your body. This means your amygdala has switched on and is trying to protect you from danger.

But . . . you're in a theater. There is no *real* danger!

Your mind thinks about what's happening to your body, and then makes a judgment that it's a false alarm. You're still in a movie theater. Still in a cozy chair. Still safe. You *decide* that you don't need to *feel* afraid.

THE MOVIE THEATER TECHNIQUE

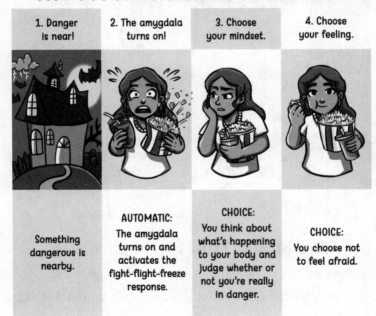

1. Danger is near!	2. The amygdala turns on!	3. Choose your mindset.	4. Choose your feeling.
Something dangerous is nearby.	AUTOMATIC: The amygdala turns on and activates the fight-flight-freeze response.	CHOICE: You think about what's happening to your body and judge whether or not you're really in danger.	CHOICE: You choose not to feel afraid.

We repeat: you ***decide*** that you don't need to feel afraid.

This is the decision we want you to make every time you panic when there is no real danger. If you're hanging out in school and you start to panic, remember the movie theater technique. Just because your amygdala kicks into high gear doesn't mean you need to feel afraid or panicky. Your body might feel uncomfortable, but you are safe. There is no danger. Once you make this judgment, panic gets crushed.

Now, we're not going to tell you that getting through panic or extreme anxiety is easy, but we are going to tell you it is doable and we know you can do it. And since we've done it ourselves, we're really familiar with the main challenge: panicky feelings make your body feel really **uncomfortable.** We get it. But feeling uncomfortable is just that—uncomfortable.

We want you to start using the movie theater technique in panic situations, which basically means shift your mindset. Shift your mindset to remind yourself that you're not in danger; you're just uncomfortable, and the feelings will pass.

Try these exercises!

1. **Choose your mindset!** While your body might panic, your mind can decide that the situation is a false alarm and you don't have to feel afraid. One of the best ways to do this is to have the right mindset. Here's a helpful mindset statement: "My body is panicking and it's uncomfortable, but I'm safe and this will pass." What can each of these kids say to themselves to help them get through their panic? Write a mindset statement for each.

Kai is thinking about soccer tryouts and starts to panic.

Mike is going into a party where he deosn't know many people. He starts to panic.

Hoda is worried the food she eats might trigger her allergies. She starts to panic.

Alana is making a sandwich at home. She has no idea why, but she starts to panic.

2. **Ride the wave!** Just like a wave, the feelings of panic will crash over you and then pass. Once you realize that panic is a false alarm, then you know you're merely uncomfortable but totally safe. You can practice riding the wave by visualizing yourself on a surfboard and repeating a mantra or a saying that will help you shift your mindset. Check out the next pages for sample mantras, and then flip the page again and write in your own. Don't forget to draw yourself on the surfboard, riding the wave!

3. Have fun with it! Sometimes what happens to our body when we panic can *feel* scary. We feel like our body can't handle what's happening. It's helpful to remember that sometimes you have those *exact* same experiences when you're having fun! Below, write in activities or situations you can think of that create the same body experience as panic but aren't scary.

Feeling	Fun!	Feeling	Fun!
Dizzy	Example: I get dizzy when I twirl around for fun!	Heart Racing	Example: My heart races when I see a scary movie for fun!
Sweating		Nausea	
Cold Sweat		Hot Flash	
Tingling		Feeling Unreal	
Trembling		Short of Breath	

4. Feelings have purpose! Each of the feelings you have when you panic may be related to the fight, flight, or freeze response (or the 3Fs) that you learned about in chapter 4. Which scary feelings line up with the survival feelings below?

Mega Muscles

Boosted by extra oxygen and energy, your important muscles tense, ready to fight, flee, or freeze. Arm and leg muscles become extra-powerful, letting you run faster and fight harder.

Hyper Heartbeat

Your heart ramps up the rate at which it pumps, shooting blood to all the organs essential to fighting, fleeing, or freezing.

Supercool

Your body hair stands on end and you sweat, keeping you cool, calm, and collected.

Extreme Energy

Your liver pumps out amazing amounts of sugar, powering up your body.

Bionic Brainpower

Your brain focuses only on crucial information, just like a robot. You target only the source of danger, helping you react and make decisions ultrafast.

Supersensitive Sight

Your eyes home in on a potential threat by switching off all receptors except the ones focused straight ahead. Your pupils open wide, letting in more light. Your eyesight becomes super sharp and supersensitive.

Boosted Breathing

Your lungs suck in extra oxygen, giving you super energy and powering up your muscles.

Supersonic Senses

Your senses of hearing, touch, sight, and smell become ultra-alert to danger. You can react in less than a millisecond to any sign of a threat.

KEY TAKEAWAYS

- When we're Iced, we try to avoid anything that makes us worried or anxious. Avoidance makes feelings of worry worse.

- When your body goes into a fear or panic response, that doesn't mean you feel the emotion of fear. Fear is a choice you can make.

- When you panic, remember that you're uncomfortable but you aren't necessarily in danger.

PART THREE
SUPERPOWERED

You made it to part three of the book! We are so proud of you! By now you have an understanding of how you lost your superpowers. You may be starting to get control of your worries and anxieties. If you're still struggling, please be patient with yourself; this process takes time, and you are not alone.

But we do think it's time. You're ready. We're going to, once again, become *SUPERPOWERED*!

Every superhero has a set of powers. And if you watch superhero movies or read comics, you know that each hero gets their power from somewhere. There's something that *fuels* the power. For some heroes, that fuel is a bite from a radioactive bug. For others, it's some laboratory experiment gone wrong. One of the most famous heroes of all gets his power from the sun. Your superpowers need fuel as well. In this last section, we're going to tell you all about what it takes to get your superpowers back, AND we're going to reveal the secret ingredient that fuels each of your abilities.

Are you ready? Let's get *SUPERPOWERED*!

CHAPTER 10
PRESENT

Quinn's Journal,
July 22, 11:11 a.m.

Something crazy happened today. I always
hear people use the phrase "out-of-body
experience." I never knew what that
meant, but now I think I do!

Wait. . . . I'm not going to understand
this when I read it later. I have to back up
for a sec. . . .

Mom always tells me I'm a good friend to
people, like, a good listener and helpful and
stuff, and she says I should try to do that
for myself when I'm stressed out, which is
actually a lot of the time. But . . . a friend
to myself? What does that even MEAN?! I
understood the part about being good to
others. Like when Amir left his lunch in his

stepdad's car and he was so mad at
himself. I told him we all do stuff like
that and I gave him half my lunch. And
last week, Jess was really stressed about
some big tests coming up. What she said
made sense. . . . Those tests were gonna
be HARD! But I didn't let her worry make
me worry, too. I just listened and gave her
some advice. So yeah, when my friends have
a problem, I can be there for them. BUT
being a friend to myself? I couldn't even
picture that. It made no sense.

    Until today. Today was different. I was
having some worried thoughts, and I could
feel the flip-flops starting in my stomach.
Instead of getting all worked up, I took
a few deep breaths, and suddenly it was
like I was outside of myself. Everything
kinda slowed down, and it's like . . . This
is strange. . . . I could SEE my thoughts
and feelings. I know, strange. Then I
started talking to myself. I told myself the
thoughts probably weren't true and to just
let them pass by. It's like . . . it's like I
was able to be my own friend. I wouldn't
tell Mom, but sometimes . . . okay, a lot of
times . . . she's just right.

When you need a great friend, they drop what they're doing to be there for you, right? That's what Quinn does. When her friends are struggling, she tunes in, supports them, and does one of the hardest things of all. . . . She sees what they're going through and doesn't judge what they do or say. She understands that everyone goes through tough times. Like when Amir forgot his lunch, she didn't make him feel bad about it. It also sounds like she can empathize with her friends' feelings, but she's able to keep enough distance that she doesn't go through the feelings herself. Like when Jess was worried about that test, Quinn listened and understood without getting worried herself. Quinn basically tries to *notice* what her friends are going through. Quinn is Mindful. And when she had worried thoughts of her own, she turned that Mindfulness inward.

"Mindfulness" means bringing your focus to the present moment, and accepting your thoughts and feelings for what they are without judging them, trying to change them, or expecting them to be different.

Mindfulness is the secret fuel that activates your super-power of being **Present**.

Quinn wasn't always Mindful. Like so many of us, she used to struggle with time traveling (remember chapter 5?), What-iffing, and all kinds of worried thoughts. After using some exercises to help squash her time-traveling habits (some of the same exercises we've shared with you), Quinn slowly transformed herself from a worrier to a noticer. And you can do the same!

Being a Noticer

If you're no longer spending too much time worrying about the past and future, you'll start to find yourself with more time to focus on what's going on in the present moment, and more opportunities to notice what's happening here and now. There's no bad time to try being a noticer. Start with a simple exercise: close your eyes, take a deep breath, and without looking, see how many things you can notice. Wait, why are you still reading? Go ahead. Close your eyes, and try it. We'll still be here when you come back.

So, what did you notice? The way the chair felt on your body? The smell of dinner cooking in the kitchen? Sounds of cars going by outside? Did you notice anything going on in your own body? Are you cold? Warm? Hungry? Tired?

Let's take it a step further. Next time you're in the lunch line at school or waiting to order something at a restaurant, close your eyes and take a deep breath. And when you open your eyes again, take in as much of the moment as you can, free of any judgment or emotion. What conversations can you hear around you? What does the lunch tray or plate feel like on your fingers? What does the food smell like?

These exercises are meant to show you what it can mean to be a noticer. Remember how good Quinn was at noticing what was going on with the people around her? It's part of what made her such a good friend. It allowed her to see them and interact without judgment. But then she took Mindfulness even further when she was able to step outside herself and notice *what was going on with her own thoughts and feelings*. She was able to console herself, recognize her own struggle, and offer herself some advice. And you're going to be able to do the same.

Exercise: Write a few challenging thoughts on a piece of paper, things like "I'm horrible at everything" or "I'm never going to sleep tonight." Now hold that paper really, really close to your face for at least a minute. Ready? Go!

How did that feel? Pretty hard to focus on anything but the paper and those thoughts, right?

This is how most of us view our own thoughts and feelings. What we're trying to show you is something researchers call "cognitive fusion." Those science-y words basically mean that your thoughts are tied, Velcroed, glued, stuck, or generally fused to you. When thoughts are fused to you, they have a huge influence on how you feel and behave.

As we discussed, by practicing Mindfulness, Quinn was able to go from being fused to her thoughts to being a noticer. When you're a noticer, you notice your own experience just like you would notice a friend's experience, or anything else around you. When you're a noticer, you are not trying to change your thoughts. You're just watching or noticing them. Noticing helps create a space between you and your thoughts. Noticing helps *you* give *yourself* advice. In other words, you become your own best friend.

Still have that paper with your thoughts on it from the earlier exercise? Hold the paper out in front of you and look at it. This is how we want you to think about your thoughts. They are still there, but they are separate from you. There is space between you and your thoughts. This way, your thoughts aren't gone, but they aren't the only thing you focus on.

Exercise: You can start becoming a noticer right away by changing some of your sentences. For example, you can go from "I'm gonna bomb the tryouts next week!" to "*I notice I'm having the thought that* I'm gonna bomb the try-outs next week!" Try it with a thought or feeling you're having right now. Put the words "I notice I'm having a thought (or feeling) that . . ." and then insert your thought or feeling.

More on Thoughts

Ever wonder where all our thoughts come from in the first place? Think of them like pieces of data or information we've collected through our lives.

THOUGHTS = WHO WE ARE

THOUGHTS = DATA WE HAVE PICKED UP

Where does this data come from? Some of our data comes from our parents, the shows we watch, the friends we hang out with, and the social media we consume. When you become a noticer of your thoughts, you will see that a lot of the data comes from others. Here's the great thing: once you understand that many of your thoughts are not from within you, something amazing happens—you realize you have a CHOICE!

AHA! MOMENT: *I don't have to believe all my thoughts. I can* **choose** *the thoughts I believe and care about. Thoughts are not commands I have to obey, are not always true, and don't always need my attention.*

Kids always tell us they can't help thinking worried thoughts. No problem! You don't have to change your thoughts—you just need to *change your relationship* with them. You can befriend some thoughts and let the others go.

How do you know if you should befriend a thought? Stop what you're doing right now and observe your thoughts. Choose one thought and answer these three questions about the thought:

1. Is this thought useful to me right now?
2. Does this thought match my values?
3. Is this thought something I truly believe in?

If you answer no to any of these questions, let the thought pass by. Here are two ways to let them pass by:

    a. Karaoke your thoughts! Take your What-iffing thought and sing it to the tune of a popular nursery rhyme like "London Bridge Is Falling Down."

    b. Practice simply visualizing your thoughts and feelings pass by.

Get Present!

Remember, you came into this world with the superpower of being **Present.** You could stare at a bug walking across the sidewalk for half an hour. You could spend all day picking the perfect flowers to tie together as a gift for your mom. You could go from crying in pain to squealing with joy in a split second! You could do all of this because you soaked in your experience from moment to moment. You lived in the present. Everything you've read in this chapter was a way to reactivate your superpower of being **Present.** Now you're going to supersize your superpower with these Mindfulness exercises! It's really a lot simpler than you imagine. Go ahead and grab a cushion if you'd like, or just sit right on the floor with your legs crossed.

Try these exercises!

1. Breathing meditation

    a. Set a timer on a phone or clock for three minutes.

    b. Begin breathing in through your nose and out through your mouth. Don't worry about the idea of deep breathing; instead, try to exhale for as long as you can (while still feeling comfortable).

    c. Try focusing on your breath as your chest and/or belly rises and falls.

d. Place one hand on your chest and one hand on your belly. Notice any movements there as you breathe.

e. Pay attention to your breath going in through your nose and out through your nose. As you do this, your thoughts will come and go. Just notice them coming and going, and let them pass by.

f. Thoughts are normal, so don't be bothered if you have them. If you get distracted, all you need to do is return your awareness to your breath in the present moment. Over and over if necessary.

2. Hands meditation

a. Clap your hands in front of you five times. Then rub the palms of your hands together quickly for fifteen seconds.

b. With your hands in front of you, palms still touching, slowly create space between your hands. Pull them away from each other about an inch.

c. Do you notice any sensations in your hands? Any tingling? How about between your hands?

d. Slowly bring your hands away from each other a little bit more. Imagine invisible strings connecting them. Can you feel the connection between your hands? What do you feel?

After you've tried one of the Mindfulness
meditations, think about what you noticed.

Circle anything you felt:

- Tingly sensations around your body
- Sleepiness
- Fatigue
- Your thoughts were zipping through your mind
  at a hundred miles per second
- A sense of calm and quiet
- Fidgetiness
- Restlessness
- Anxiety
- Frustration around being anxious
- Your mind tuning out

If you are anything like us, you probably felt
a bit of all the sensations and emotions listed
above. Do not worry if this is how you felt.
Meditation is about progress, not perfection.
Work on these exercises for a few minutes
each day and note how your experience
changes.

- Being more Mindful allows us to be **Present** and observe everything around us in that moment, including ourselves, our own physical sensations, and our own emotions!

- When we can observe ourselves, we can be friends to ourselves.

- We can make decisions about which thoughts to listen to and embrace, and which thoughts to acknowledge but allow to pass by.

CHAPTER 11

ORIGINAL

Who Is She?

When she was younger, she wanted to be a novelist. Her parents, knowing how difficult it was to pay bills and make a living as a writer, pushed her to study something more practical. She didn't listen. There was a voice inside her that she couldn't ignore, so she went for a degree in classic literature.

Seven years after graduating college, she was divorced, unemployed, raising a child alone, depressed, and she said, "as poor as it is possible to be . . . without being homeless. The fears that my parents had had for me, and that I had had for myself, had both come to pass, and by every usual standard, I was the biggest failure I knew." She was filled with so much doubt and sadness. Should she have ignored that voice that told her to write? Should she have listened instead to everyone around her?

Despite these horrible doubts, despite the advice of loved ones, despite the odds against her, and despite her failures, that inner voice kept talking. So, she wrote a book and sent it to a dozen publishers. They all rejected it, but still that inner voice told her to keep going. She tried again. And again. And eventually she found someone willing to publish her book.

Who is she? Her name is J. K. Rowling, and she wrote the Harry Potter series.

"We do not need magic to transform the world. We carry all the power we need inside ourselves already. We have the power to imagine better."

Do you remember all the way back in chapter 1 when we talked about your superpower of being **Original**? For the first few years of your life, you were completely unaware of the opinions of others. Even around other kids, you did whatever you wanted: built a kingdom using blankets and sheets; pretended you were a dinosaur; sang a concert of gibberish. Things the other kids were doing didn't influence your ideas or your actions. From the way you dressed to the foods you ate to the music you played . . . you were always being you. All of this happened because your **Originality** was fueled by a strong Inner Voice.

The Inner Voice is the secret fuel that activates your superpower of being **Original.**

Inner Voice → Original

What's an Inner Voice?

Let's do a quick thought experiment. Pretend an alien is on a galactic mission to get to know as many species as possible. . . . She has about 250 billion planets to visit! She lands on Earth with only a minute to chat. You're the first person she sees, there's not another person in sight, and she asks, "What are you?"

You say you're human, but it's clear she meant to ask a different question. "Oh, yes, you are hooman, I do know. But *WHO* are you?"

Good question, you think. *Who am I?*

You look around. Still just you and the alien. Everything you say is just between the two of you. So, maybe you say something like, "My name is Jackson. I like baseball cards and family dinners—especially dessert. I like hanging out with friends, but I also like alone time. When nobody is listening, I like to sing songs that I make up and make no sense.

"My heart says..."

DID YOU KNOW?

The heart is amazing. It weighs ten ounces on average and is about the size of a fist, yet it does much more than just pump oxygen and nutrient-rich blood throughout the body. In fact, research shows that the heart can learn, processes information, and has short- and long-term memory. Not only that, the heart is in constant two-way communication with the brain, sending more information to the brain than the other way around. The heart influences our choices. The heart influences how we think and feel. The term "heart-brain" was coined to recognize that the human heart has its own brain independent of the one in your head.

It's no wonder that when you've had a decision to make, you might have heard people ask "What does your heart say?" or suggest that "your heart knows best."

I worry about the environment, so I'm in the Green Club at school. Oh, and since you're probably not going to tell anyone, I also like math . . . a lot. Even though it's not very cool."

And with that, the alien nods, takes some notes, flashes a four-finger wave, and hops back onto her ship.

You can do this exercise on a separate sheet of paper. Knowing that nobody else will see, write down who YOU are. Then when you're done, if you'd like, fold up the paper and keep it for yourself.

What can you learn from this thought exercise? When you privately answer the question "Who are you?" you get clues about what you care about. And what you care about helps you to hear your Inner Voice. But what exactly is an Inner Voice?

Whether you call it a gut feeling, a hunch, an inkling, a sense, your inner wisdom, or your intuition, they are all names for your Inner Voice. Your Inner Voice is the truth that lives inside you. The voice speaks to you when you need to make decisions, especially difficult ones. This voice might show up as words or images in your head. Your Inner Voice may show up as a feeling in your body—a lot of times this feeling is in your heart or stomach.

Your Inner Voice gives you immediate opinions about things. It sounds like this:

This is a good idea.

I have a bad feeling about this.

I really care about this.

I'm curious about this.

I would never do that.

I believe in this.

I dream about this.

This is exciting to me!

Your Inner Voice Is a Guide

Your Inner Voice is your unique GPS system that guides your actions. When you follow your Inner Voice, your actions match the voice you hear inside, and you show up in the world with the superpower of being **Original.**

Inner Voices in Action

In 2007, two Canadian high school students named David Shepherd and Travis Price saw one of their classmates being bullied for wearing a pink shirt. Even though it might have been easier to do nothing, their Inner Voices spoke clearly, saying: This isn't right. You need to do something to help. *They listened to their Inner Voices, and help they did.*

David and Travis bought fifty pink shirts, passed them out to as many students as they could, and told everyone to wear them to school the next day. They didn't know who would actually do it; they just knew that their Inner Voices were telling them they had to try.

The following morning, hundreds of kids showed up dressed in pink. The word spread throughout Canada and sparked something called "Pink Shirt Day" across the country. David's and Travis's courage also inspired the United Nations

to establish an Anti-Bullying Day, which is recog-
nized by countries around the world!

David and Travis are an inspiration for sure, but whether you believe it or not, your Inner Voice is just as strong as theirs. In fact, we all come into this world with a crystal-clear Inner Voice that reminds us of our **Originality,** of who we are, and of what we believe in. So, what happens? Noise from the outside world filters in. The opinions of others, what we see online, hear in music, and watch on TV, what we believe everyone else is doing, the culture we live in, the systems we enter (like school), and all the hundreds and thousands of rules and "shoulds" create enough noise to drown out our Inner Voice and make us forget who we truly are. We forget our **Originality.**

It's pretty easy to tell if your Inner Voice has been drowned out. Your Inner Voice and your actions DO NOT MATCH!

Wake Up, Inner Voice!

Luckily, just like your superpowers, your Inner Voice is still totally intact. You just need to wake it up and allow it to be heard! Let's give that a try with an exercise on the next page.

In the left column are phrases to help you remember what your Inner Voice is trying to say. Finish the sentences we started for you. On the right, list some actions you can take to support that voice.

INNER VOICE says...	Supporting Actions:
I care about my family.	I spend quality time with my family.
I care about...	
I believe...	
I would change the world like this...	
I'm curious about...	
I value...	
I'm excited by...	

Seriously, Inner Voice, WAKE UP!

You didn't think it was going to be *that* easy to wake up your Inner Voice, did you? We want to make sure you have a clear pathway back to the wisdom that lies within you. To do that, try taking these three action steps:

Step #1: Keep It Real . . . with Yourself

Being **Original** takes honesty, and honesty takes guts. Even if you can't be honest with others, you need to be honest *with yourself.* We know that it's scary to confront others with the truth sometimes. But by avoiding this confrontation, we end up lying to ourselves and we start to lose track of who we are. Start being true to yourself by asking these kinds of questions when you face a decision:

> *How do I really feel about this?*
> *Do I really want to go on this trip?*
> *Do I really want to talk in this moment?*
> *Do I really want to say yes to this invitation?*

Once you become honest about how you feel, chances are that the honesty will spill outward. And once that happens, you might run into conflict. This brings us to step two.

Step #2: Argue More

Are we actually telling you to get into more arguments? Yeah, I guess we are.

How often have you not spoken up, or not shared an opinion, because you knew that others would disagree? Listening to your own Inner Voice and exercising your superpower of being **Original** usually means not hiding your opinions. Go ahead and share them. Often when you share your opinions, others see a chance to share theirs, and debates—or even arguments—may start. This isn't always a bad thing! You may learn something new! Each of your ideas may evolve into something better. Sure, it would be easy to hide your opinions, but hiding your Inner Voice all the time also hides who you really are from the world. Orville and Wilbur Wright, inventors of the first successful airplane, show us what this looks like:

Step #3: Take Action

Your Inner Voice is strengthened by taking action. Listen to your voice and act on it. Here's what this looks like:

Try these exercises!

1. **Give out a few keys to your heart.** Sometimes your Inner Voice gets information from the outside and it's not just noise; it's useful. How do you know who or what you should let in? You choose. We want you to choose five people whose opinions you value and trust very much. Imagine giving each of them a key that allows access to your Inner Voice. For example, giving someone a key means you are willing to share with them your innermost truths. They can support you when you need help making a big decision or when you're going through challenges. *Not* giving a key to someone is also

important. If you feel peer pressure, hurt, or noise from someone without a key, you've already decided that they will not affect your Inner Voice.

Who will you give your keys to? Write on the keys the names of those who get a key to your Inner Voice.

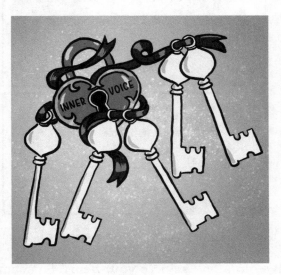

2. **Take chances.** Follow your Inner Voice and who you really are instead of following a possible outcome. For example, let's say your Inner Voice is telling you to take a chance and perform one of your own songs in the talent show. You can double-check that it's *your* Inner Voice speaking by putting your hand on your heart, closing your eyes, and seeing what you feel. Knowing and following your voice helps you take risks. Following the outcome can lead to avoiding risk. Here's the difference:

FOLLOWING YOUR INNER VOICE:	FOLLOWING THE OUTCOME:
"I want to perform in the talent show."	"I want to win."
"I have a song that I've already started writing that I think is perfect."	"I want to make sure it's the best performance ever."
"I think this is gonna be a ton of fun."	"I want to make sure everyone loves it."

3. **Who said it?** Can you guess what famous person made the following statements?

"I didn't fit in in high school, and I felt like a freak."

"This is really who I am, and it took a long time to be okay with that."

"It is your right to choose what you do and don't do. It is your right to choose what you believe in and what you don't believe in. You are not here to be a puppet."

"Part of my identity is saying no to things I don't want to do. . . . 'I'm not taking that picture. I'm not going to that event. . . .' You look in the mirror and you're like 'YES . . . I know that person. . . . That person has integrity.'"

Each of those quotes came from Lady Gaga, who personally battled with the desire to Camouflage before embracing her superpower of being **Original.**

"Sometimes in life you don't always feel like a winner, but that doesn't mean you're not a winner. You want to be like yourself."
— Lady Gaga

4. **What does your inner voice say?** You can practice listening to your Inner Voice by asking yourself questions and listening or feeling inside yourself for the answers. Try out the examples that follow:

SCENE

A friend of yours has broken his leg and needs to stay inside for recess. Everyone else gets on their coats to run outside and play soccer, which is usually the best part of your day. You stand in the doorway, looking at your friend sitting alone, and then you look at the last of the other kids slipping away. What does your Inner Voice say? What do you do?

INNER VOICE

_____

_____

_____

_____

_____

SCENE

You're working on a group project with three other students. You're supposed to present on the solar system, and everyone else keeps insisting there are nine planets, even though you know there are only eight. (Pluto is a dwarf planet!) Still, it's three against one, and you're two minutes from getting in front of the class. What does your Inner Voice say? What do you do?

INNER VOICE

_____

_____

_____

_____

_____

SCENE

Your favorite aunt is babysitting for the night. Before your mom left, she told you "No video games" and that you needed to read for an hour. After dinner, your aunt fires up the television and hands you a controller. "You ready to take me on?" she asks. You know your aunt won't tell, but still . . . What does your Inner Voice say? What do you do?

INNER VOICE

_____

_____

_____

_____

_____

SCENE

You're really tired after a long week of school. Nothing sounds better than to go home, eat a frozen pizza, and watch a movie with your dad. But your best friend is having people over. "Why would you want to go home? Don't you like coming to my house?" she asks. You just don't feel in the mood, but you also have some serious FOMO. What does your Inner Voice say? What do you do?

INNER VOICE

_____

_____

_____

_____

_____

KEY TAKEAWAYS

- Your Inner Voice is unique, speaks to you, and guides your decisions.

- When you listen to your Inner Voice, you're fueling your superpower of being **Original.**

- Your Inner Voice might lead you out of your comfort zone, into arguments, or to take more risks, but if you trust it, it will never lead you wrong.

CHAPTER 12
WHOLE

Gia started playing with dolls when she was very young. She got her first when she turned two, and after that, she didn't let a birthday or holiday go by without letting everyone know that dolls and accessories for them were at the top of her list of presents. Her friends had them, too, and sometimes the girls acted out their stories together.

But then, as Gia got older, something happened. Her friends suddenly decided that dolls were for babies. Gia didn't think that, but knowing that her friends would tease her, she stopped talking about dolls, and when people visited her home, she hid every doll she owned in the back of her closet. It was only when she was alone that they'd come out again, and for years she continued to use them to tell stories, walking them around an imaginary world, posing them, having them act out scenes she'd written in her head. Still, she felt like a weirdo—like she and her little secret habit didn't Belong anywhere.

That all changed in eighth grade. Gia's class was assigned a video project in which the students, in small groups, needed to write a script, film it, and show it to the class. The rest of her class was at a loss as to how to position actors, where to put the camera, or even how to tell a convincing story. Gia watched everyone in her group struggle for an entire class period, then decided to step in and volunteer herself as the director. The next day, she came to class with a box of her dolls, and together with her classmates, she used them to stage a scene and plan the positioning and movements of characters. The students even used someone's cell phone to experiment with camera placement. By the end of the day, they had their whole video project planned, and Gia was on her way to learning that she and her passions really did Belong somewhere.

You've now activated your superpowers of being **Present** and **Original.** Your thoughts and feelings can't hold you back. Your Inner Voice is like the North Star guiding your actions. You're ready to be a pioneer, to invent, and to innovate. You're ready to take on the world! But where do you unleash your new superpowers?

Maybe your Inner Voice is telling you that you love giant pandas. In fact, there's a screening of a giant panda documentary that you really want to go to this weekend, but zero friends want to go with you, and that doesn't feel so great. Maybe you love pop music from the 1990s, but your sister gives you a *Not in a million years* look when you ask if she'll practice some pop dance moves with you. Sure, you can hear your Inner Voice and believe in it, which makes you **Original,** but why use that superpower if you feel like you can't ever share, or even talk about, who you really are? What good is it when you feel like you don't fit in anywhere?

About Fitting In . . .

We all want to feel accepted, and we work hard to do it, but sometimes we change ourselves in ways that don't feel good, ways that might feel fake. We learned about this in chapter 6 when we talked about Camouflaging. Of course, we're not doing that anymore, but that doesn't mean we don't want people to understand us and accept us. We still want to have friends and feel comfortable in social situations without having to fight our way into a group. We want people to "get" us. Without feeling loved and accepted, we can never really feel **Whole.**

We want to ask you something. To feel loved and accepted, do you really need to *fit in*? Is acceptance really about trying to match what other people want you to be? We think what you're really longing for isn't fitting in but is actually Belonging. We're not just being technical about words; these are two different ways to live life.

Fitting in is about changing yourself to "fit" a situation.

Belonging is about showing up as who you are, quirks and all, and feeling loved and accepted.

FITTING IN	BELONGING

Changing your behavior to be accepted

Changing your opinions to be accepted

Changing yourself in a way that feels inauthentic or fake to be accepted

Showing up as who you are, flaws and all, and still being accepted

How Do You Feel Like You Belong?

When you can clearly hear your Inner Voice, you've activated your superpower of being **Original.** When you're able to take that voice and show it to others, including friends, family, and other groups—and even show it to yourself—then you've activated your superpower of being **Whole.** The secret fuel that drives this superpower is Belonging.

Belonging → Whole

The most amazing thing about Belonging is that you have a lot of control over the process. It begins with you and how you see yourself. You need to fall in love with the person in the mirror. We know it's easier said than done. But don't worry; we haven't forgotten that it's our job to give you some tips on how to do it.

The Practice of Belonging

When you want to get better at a new game or sport, you take your raw talent and add effort and practice. Believe it or not, you can do the same thing with Belonging. You probably already feel a sense of Belonging in some ways (this is your raw talent), and there are practices you can do to boost this feeling (this is the effort).

DID YOU KNOW?

Not only does it feel good to build a sense of Belonging, but it's good for your health as well!

In the 1950s, scientists discovered a group of super-healthy people in a small town in Pennsylvania called Roseto. Like, unnaturally healthy. See, this was before the invention of cholesterol medicine and other strategies to prevent heart disease. Across the US, there was an epidemic of heart attacks. But not in Roseto. Almost no one in Roseto under the age of fifty showed symptoms of heart disease, and over the age of sixty-five, they had heart disease at about half the rate of every surrounding community.

The studies began. What made these people so healthy? Were they smoking less? No. Eating healthier? One of their common meals was meatballs fried in lard, so we're going to say a no on that one as well. After years of research, scientists found that what kept the Rosetans heart healthy was their social connections. Everyone in Roseto felt a sense of Belonging. Rosetans visited with each other. They lived in multi-generational homes. They ate meals together. While families were independent, they relied on the greater community for support. It was this social structure that insulated Rosetans from the health dangers of the modern world.

Let's start by figuring out the amazing ways you already Belong.

Of all the truths we've dropped in this book, we want you to pay special attention to this one: you are incredible, amazing, and beautiful right now, in this very moment, just the way you are. You are full of strengths. We're not just telling you this to make you feel good. Our experience with kids tells us it's true. And so does science. You just need help *seeing* your own strengths. To see yourself clearly, we're giving you a gift— SuperVision Glasses.

These glasses are going to help you see yourself as we see you. Check out these examples of ways that using them can change the way you feel about the person in the mirror.

Original thought: "I think too much about stuff."

SuperVision Glasses: "I have an awesome imagination."

Science: People who overthink often have great imaginations. You are able to see situations in new and inventive ways.

Original thought: "I'm kinda sensitive."

SuperVision Glasses: "I'm a great friend with a lot of empathy."

Science: When you are sensitive to your own emotions, you can turn this power outward. This makes you an ace at seeing how others feel and being a great friend to them.

Original thought: "I'm a little quiet and don't like big crowds."

SuperVision Glasses:
"I'm an amazing listener."

Science: You may feel overwhelmed or tired at a big, noisy party, but you love spending time catching up with very close friends. You are a very good listener, making close, often lifelong friendships.

Original thought: "I'm a slow decision maker."

SuperVision Glasses:
"I make a great leader."

Science: You take into account the possibility of multiple outcomes when making a decision—a characteristic of a great leader.

Time to put on your SuperVision Glasses and discover your strengths! On the next page, write in your original thoughts, followed by SuperVision thoughts.

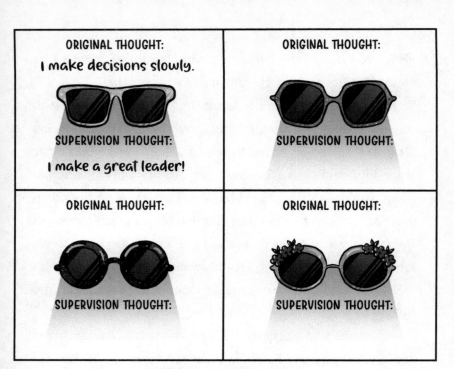

ORIGINAL THOUGHT:
I make decisions slowly.

SUPERVISION THOUGHT:
I make a great leader!

ORIGINAL THOUGHT:

SUPERVISION THOUGHT:

ORIGINAL THOUGHT:

SUPERVISION THOUGHT:

ORIGINAL THOUGHT:

SUPERVISION THOUGHT:

It Takes Just One

It's hard when you feel like you're being guided by your Inner Voice, speaking your truth, but no one really gets you or agrees with you. Okay, that's not completely correct. . . . It's not just hard. It stinks. It can feel like living in a town where nobody speaks your language.

Do you have opinions that nobody else seems to agree with? Maybe you think things like, *I LOVE lima beans.* Or *I like watching house remodeling shows.* Or *I'd rather sit and read instead of going to a birthday party.*

Whatever your opinions may be, sometimes you'll have one that isn't "popular." Maybe you won't find anyone to agree with you. And when your opinion is totally different from everyone else's, you don't just feel alone; you also find it hard to be yourself in front of others. And science proves that!

But before we share the fascinating research, we want to remind you of two things. First, your superpower of being **Original** has been activated, and you can hear your Inner Voice loud and clear. You don't need to pretend to be something you're not, or say you like something even when you don't. Second, remember that there is no greater sense of Belonging you will ever get than Belonging to yourself. We know this might be a hard idea to swallow (at any age!), but it's really powerful, and we can't leave it out of the discussion. You Belong to *you*.

Now back to the science. This one blows our minds! In the 1950s, a man named Solomon Asch conducted a now-famous experiment. It showed the effect of feeling alone with your beliefs. Imagine you're part of the experiment. You walk into a room with six other people. At the front of the room is an image that looks something like this:

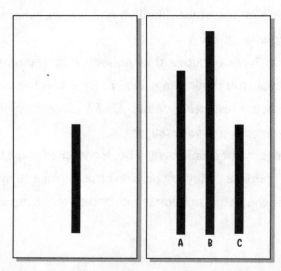

The researcher says, "Look at the line on the left. Now look at the three lines on the right. Pick the line on the right that is the same length as the line on the left."

You think it's a vision test. You look carefully at all the lines. *That's easy,* you say to yourself. Obviously the answer is C. But you need to wait your turn to answer.

The researcher calls on the first person. "Which line do you think is the same?"

"B," he says.

What?!? What's that guy looking at?!? But still, you have to wait.

The next person also says the answer is B. And the next. And the next. In fact, all six people before you say that the answer is B. And now the researcher comes to you. You look at the lines again. It's so clear to you that the answer is C. But . . . everyone else said B. Are you missing something? The researcher is waiting. You take a breath and you say . . .

What do you think you'd say? Before you answer, there are a few things about this experiment you need to know. First, the correct answer is *totally* obvious. If you looked at those lines and thought *C,* you were correct. Second, those other six people who walked into the room with you? They were in on the experiment! They had all been told ahead of time to say the wrong answer. Third, this wasn't a vision test. It was an experiment to see if people would hide their opinion just because of social pressure.

The scientists ran this experiment over and over again, and more than two out of three times, people said the wrong answer just to go along with the crowd. Amazing, right? But here's the real lesson: when just *one* other person chose the right answer before it was the experiment subject's turn, it made it much easier for the person to reject the crowd. This means that sometimes it only takes one other person to speak up and help you feel like you're not alone and that you can speak the truth, too.

What this tells us is that you can feel a greater sense of Belonging when you have even just one person that you feel is on your side. Keep speaking your truth from your Inner Voice and seek out that other person who believes in you and your voice. And if you're the first person brave enough to speak up, maybe you will be that one person who inspires someone else to share themselves.

"Did You See Jackie Robinson Hit That Ball?"

If ever a human was made to feel like he didn't Belong, it was Jackie Robinson. In the 1940s in America, a practice called segregation existed, where people of different races were separated in daily activities, including where they socialized, lived, and were educated. Even black baseball players and white baseball players were made to compete in separate leagues.

When the general manager of the all-white Major League Baseball team the Brooklyn Dodgers decided it was time that white players and black players played together, he knew it wouldn't be easy. He knew that it would be difficult for the white fans of the era to accept a player of color. He needed somebody strong to be the first black man in the majors. He needed someone to step up when nobody else would. The player needed to be an **Original** with a strong Inner Voice. The general manager selected Jackie Robinson, not just because he was talented but because Jackie was strong enough to withstand tens of thousands of coaches, players, and fans telling him he didn't Belong.

"I'm not concerned with your liking or disliking me...all I ask is that you respect me as a human being."
—Jackie Robinson

Jackie used every bit of his Superpower of being **Whole** to show the world that he did Belong. In his first year, he was selected as Rookie of the Year. A few years later, he batted .342 (which is REALLY good), and led the league in stolen bases, which helped earn him the league's Most Valuable Player award. In 1955, he helped lead the Dodgers to a World Series victory. But most important, because he was brave enough to stand alone, he ushered in a new era in baseball, where people of all races could love the game together.

Try these exercises!

1. **Bring down barriers.** We are all connected! Think about someone you don't feel like you're friends with— the boy in homeroom who might give you a hard time, the girl on the bus who you block from sitting next to you with your backpack, or your sibling who you fight with all the time. You are all connected. You are connected to everyone who you feel doesn't really get you and who you would never hang out with, or vice versa. You—we—are all connected.

   We're all connected not just because we're all human but because we all have common experiences, including challenges and celebrations. Think about that someone who you don't feel connected to right now. Do this exercise with that person in mind.

   Write down some struggles you think they may have, and then write down some of your own. Then write down some things you think they celebrate and write down your own things. Link together anything you see in common between your challenges and theirs, and then between your celebrations. Even if you can't find any commonality in the details, never forget you are connected because you both have challenges and you both have things you celebrate. Here's an example, and on the next pages is space to fill out your own.

Their challenges:

Their celebrations:

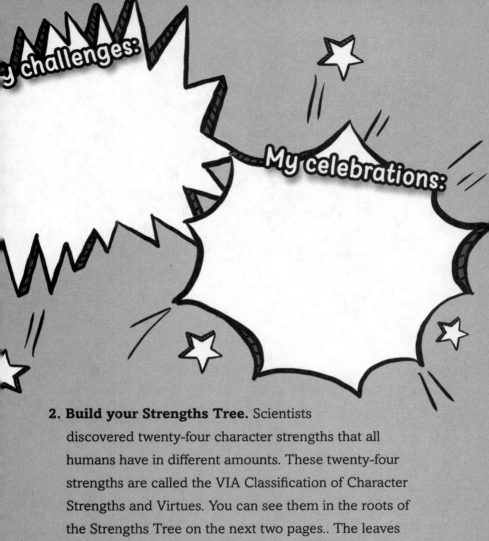

y challenges:

My celebrations:

2. **Build your Strengths Tree.** Scientists discovered twenty-four character strengths that all humans have in different amounts. These twenty-four strengths are called the VIA Classification of Character Strengths and Virtues. You can see them in the roots of the Strengths Tree on the next two pages.. The leaves of the tree show you how the strengths might show up in life. Now draw your own tree with roots and leaves. Write down at least three of your greatest strengths in the roots of the tree, and use the leaves to write how those strengths show up in your life!

3. **Belonging to your body.** It's easy to say you Belong to you, but in order to really live by those words, you have to practice *loving* and *accepting* and *celebrating* yourself just the way you are. Some of the areas where we see kids (and grown-ups!) really struggle to feel like they Belong is within their body. If you feel this way, try these exercises.

Say sorry. If you've been unkind in words or actions to your body, it's time to say sorry for treating your body poorly.

Say "I love you." Your body does incredible tasks for you day and night. Time to send love and acceptance and thank-yous to your body for helping you in all these different ways.

On the following pages, write an "I'm sorry" letter and an "I love you" letter to your body.

I'm sorry

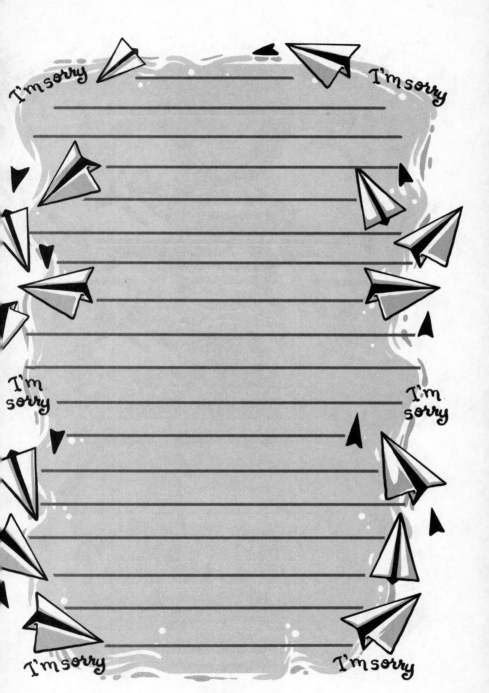

4. Loving-kindness. Loving-kindness is a meditation that helps you love and accept yourself and others. It's a really awesome way to boost your feelings of Belonging. Try this meditation first thing in the morning or before you sleep at night. Make sure you're sitting or lying down in a comfortable position.

Take a deep breath in through your nose and out through your mouth. Repeat these words:

May I be happy, healthy, and peaceful.
May I let go of sadness and bad feelings.
May I be free from anger.
May I be free from pain.
May I be free from difficulties.
May I be free from suffering.
May I be healthy, happy, and peaceful.
May I be filled with loving-kindness.
May I be at peace.

Take a deep breath in through your nose and out through your mouth. Repeat these words:

I spread this loving-kindness out.
I send love and kindness to my family.
I send love and kindness to my friends.

I send love and kindness to all humans.

May they let go of sadness and bad feelings.

May they be free from anger.

May they be free from pain.

May they be free from difficulties.

May they be free from suffering.

May they be healthy, happy, and peaceful.

May they be filled with loving-kindness.

May they be at peace.

- To feel **Whole,** we need to feel loved and accepted, but that doesn't mean changing ourselves to fit in. It means finding a true place of Belonging.

- Often it takes only one person who sees and understands us for us to achieve a sense of Belonging and to feel Whole.

CHAPTER 13
ENERGIZED

Lola walked into her guidance counselor's office, then stopped dead in her tracks. "Where's Mr. Treadwell?" she said to the strange woman sitting behind the desk. Lola hated surprises. She was already tired and didn't want to deal with any weirdness.

"Mr. Treadwell is on vacation this week. I'm filling in until he gets back. I'm Ms. Awestruck." Ms. Awestruck's hair was huge, and there was weird flute music playing in the background.

"Um, I made an appointment to go through a career planning session with Mr. Treadwell. I need to figure all this out, and I'm running out of time." Lola felt nervous and started chewing on the end of her pen. She couldn't afford to lose ground. This was serious!

"Career planning, huh? How old are you?"

"Twelve."

"Have a seat, Lola. Why don't you tell me exactly what you're planning for."

"I need to know what electives to take in high school so I get into good classes in college so I can get a good job when I graduate so I can—"

"Whoa, whoa, whoa. Slow down. That's a long road you're

describing. You've got time. Why do you feel rushed? What do you think you're going to find at the end of this race you're running?"

Lola shrugged her shoulders. She had a picture of it all in her mind. A house. A white fence. But she wasn't about to share that with Ms. Awestruck. It was a little embarrassing.

"Let me guess," said Ms. Awestruck. "A house. A white fence. Is that really what energizes you? Do any of those things mean anything to you?"

"What do you mean when you say 'mean anything'?"

"Listen, you can come back next week and do your career planning with Mr. Treadwell. That's important. But I want to do something else with our time today. We're going to focus on meaning planning."

Yes, we're here to tell you about Meaning, the secret fuel for your superpower of being **Energized.**

Meaning → Energized

We know that feeling **Energized** is important to you, so we won't delay too long. But before we get started, we just realized that this book is almost finished (sad, we know!) and we haven't talked much about superheroes. I mean, for a book titled *Superpowered,* there's been a severe lack of superhero conversation.

Where do we even start? Okay, so there's the guy with the shield. The woman with the red hair and powerful kick. The guy who dresses up like a bat. There's the woman with the superstrength and the Lasso of Truth. There's the guy who dresses up like a panther—he's got the coolest suit. Oh, but then there's our favorite superhero! The guy who can shrink himself to be super small. He's like an ant-sized man. What's his name again? We like him because even though he's super small compared to everyone else, he's still totally powerful. You're probably wondering what the ant guy has to do with anything. Tell ya what, we'll come back to that before the end

of the chapter. We promise. For now, let's focus on getting you **Energized.**

What's the Point of Anything?

We used to sit in algebra class and think, *I don't feel like doing this! What's the point?* Our parents used to ask us to make our beds every morning, and we'd say, "Why would I want to do that? Nobody is going to see it anyway!"

When you're not sure why you're doing something, it's hard to stay **Energized.** How can you stay motivated to do anything if you don't know what the point is? And, unfortunately, we've even felt that way about certain "big picture" things in life. Like, why am I doing this? Is it about getting a good job? About buying a house and having kids?

Remember the Good-Life Map we talked about in chapter 8? Remember how Fried we all get following that map? We know that spending a life pursuing happiness can create challenges. Research shows that when we go after material things, tokens of happiness, or even just happiness itself, the quest often results in the opposite. Sooner or later, if you really think that the point of life is to just be happy all the time, you're going to find your superpower of being **Energized** zapped.

There's another goal to pursue: Meaning.

Meaning is different for each of us. Meaning is what each of us sees as the value of something. What's Meaningful to us is like a fingerprint; no two people have found the exact same Meaning in life, and nobody else can tell you what things in life are Meaningful for you. Meaning is the "why" in life. Instead of happiness at the end of the Good-Life Map, you can imagine Meaning as the last destination, if you'd like. However, you need to find your own road to get there, and feel it for yourself. You need to cultivate it on your own.

Even though what makes life Meaningful is going to be different for everyone, that doesn't mean we can't try to find similarities. Which is exactly what researcher Emily Esfahani Smith did. Through her studies, she found what she calls the four pillars of meaning. These are the things that give people a sense of Meaning in life, and the things most commonly found to motivate and Energize us. They are:

BELONGING,
PURPOSE,
STORYTELLING,
and
TRANSCENDENCE.

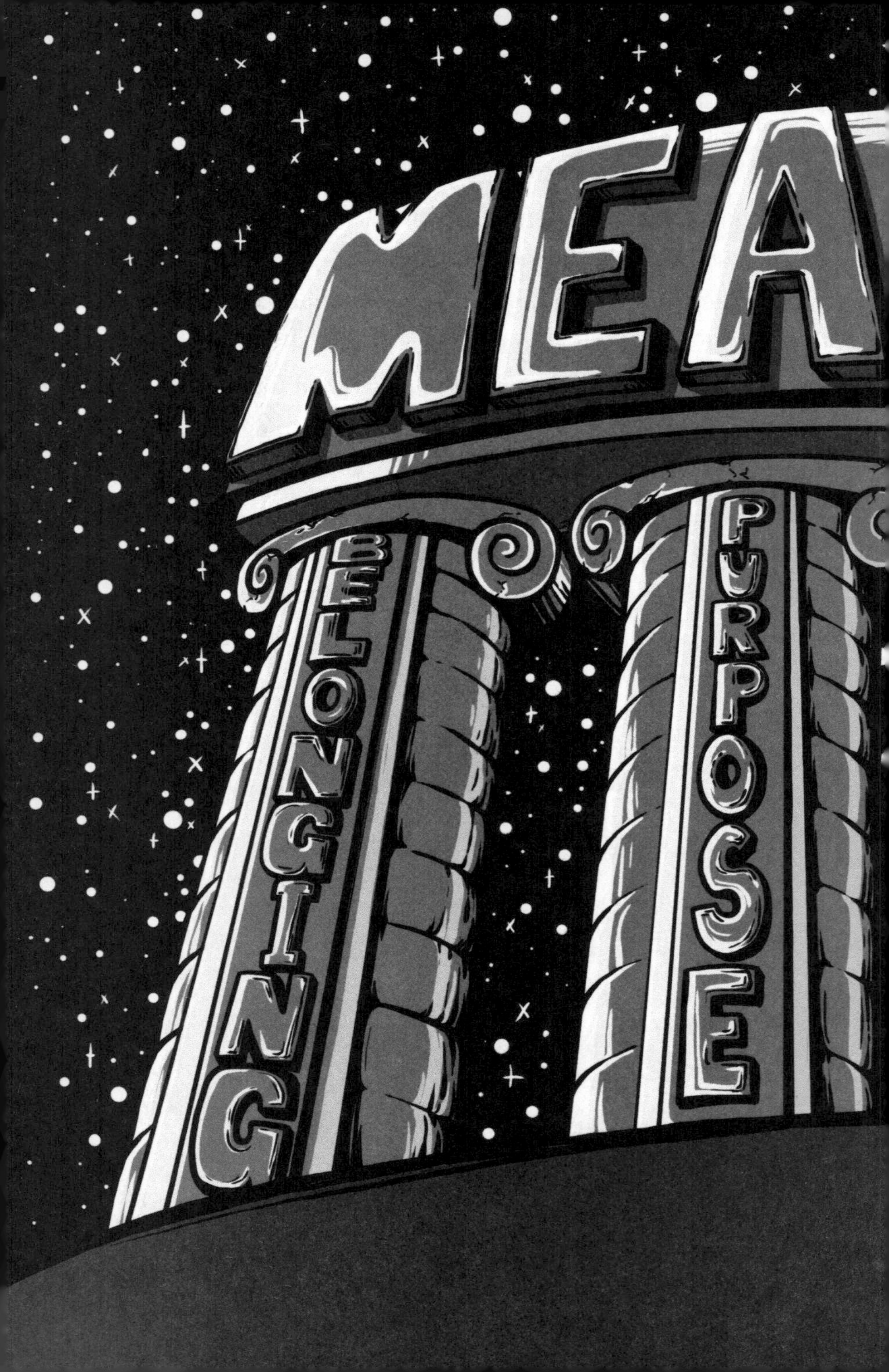
MEA
BELONGING
PURPOSE

BELONGING: If you've read this far, then you already know a lot about Belonging. We talked about it in chapter 12 when we were working on being **Whole.** Remember? Great! Everyone wants—No. Let us rephrase that. Everyone *needs*— to feel like they Belong. It is literally a biological need. But did you know that working on important relationships can be one of the foundations of a Meaningful life? It feels good to contribute to, and make a difference in, the lives of our friends. Likewise, when our friends make positive additions to our lives, it fills us with deep and lasting satisfaction. Creating and maintaining healthy relationships is Meaningful, motivating, and, yes, Energizing!

You guys mean so much to me. You make me feel like I belong.

Exercise: Think about the people in your life who are important to you. Who gives you the greatest sense of Belonging? Let's tell them. Grab a notebook or use the space below and write them a letter. Tell them about the positive impact they have on you, and how they give you a greater sense of Meaning. When you're done, take a moment to notice how it feels to tell your loved ones what they mean to you.

PURPOSE: Wait, purpose is a pillar of Meaning? But aren't Meaning and purpose the same thing? Not exactly. As we said, Meaning is what each of us sees as giving something value. Purpose, however, is having a far-reaching goal that motivates you to contribute something to the world. Maybe you discover that your purpose is volunteering at a shelter a few days a week, or cooking for people you love. Nobody else has lived your unique life. Nobody else is equipped to share exactly what's inside you. Now, that's an Energizing thought!

Exercise: Imagine yourself in the far-off future. Advances in the medical world have helped you reach the age of 151! You've lived a really Meaningful and amazing life. Now imagine that the 151-year-old version of yourself is able to use future technology to contact the present you!

Write down what future you tells you about your life.

Hello, younger me. We've lived a wonderful life. Let me tell you some things.

We contributed to the world by:

_____

_____

People appreciated what we did because:

_____

_____

It took time, but we eventually found our purpose because we:

_____

_____

_____

STORYTELLING: Yes, telling stories is an important part of a Meaningful life. Fun, right? See, humans don't deal well with disorder and chaos. We like order, logic, and easy-to-understand series of events. If we can't make sense of something, it makes us uncomfortable. Stories are structure. Stories have a beginning, middle, and end, and are often satisfying, exciting, and inspiring. So it makes perfect sense that one of the best ways to view your own life as satisfying, exciting, or inspiring is to tell a story about it!

My experience is the main reason I worked so hard to learn to swim.

When you want someone to understand who you are, you tell them stories about your life. When you want to know something about somebody else, you ask them to tell you stories about their experiences. The ways in which we begin our stories, the struggles we choose to share, and the outcomes we perceive at the end give us, and those around us, a greater sense of Meaning. The most Energizing thing about stories is that when someone is telling a good one, everyone is desperate to know what happens next. Even if we're feeling Fried, knowing that difficult events will mean more in the larger context of our lives can help us power through.

Exercise: We want you to write your life story . . . using only six words. That's right. We want you to give us a clear picture of who you are using fewer words than we're using in this sentence. To make it easier, let's start with a longer version, then shrink it down. When you're done, you should be left with a short little story that means something to you. Here's an example.

Fifty-word life story: *When I was four, my mom took me to the farm where she grew up. My grandpa was in the barn with a sick goat. I could tell it was hurting a lot, and I cried. And I never forgot that. It made me want to take care of animals.*

Twenty-word life story: *Sick animals make me sad, so I take good care of my dogs and want to be a vet someday.*

Six-word life story: *Wants to make animals' lives better.*

Fifty-word life story: _____

_____

_____

_____

_____

Twenty-word life story: _____

_____

_____

_____

Six-word life story: _____

_____

TRANSCENDENCE: This is our favorite pillar of Meaning, but it's also the most challenging to explain. It's a good thing we like challenges! Transcendence is a moment when you find yourself in awe. Transcendence is when you feel totally outside of your normal, everyday experience. You feel small (in a good way), removed from yourself, and a part of something much bigger and more important. You might even use the word "Whoaaaa!"

Transcendence, like happiness, or any other emotion, usually doesn't last, but when you feel it, you know it, and you never forget it. Some people feel transcendence when they play sports, or when they see a beautiful sunset, or when they listen to certain kinds of music, or when they learn that there are billions and billions of stars in the universe. It's a moment when you lose sight of yourself, but at the same time, the world seems to be working in harmony with you as a part of it. It's moments like this that we live for. It's moments like this that Energize us through life.

Exercise: It's really hard to just discover a transcendent experience, especially when you're reading a book! However, we found some facts that, if you think hard about them, come close to manufacturing the feeling of awe. Check these out:

- If you could build a bathtub big enough to fit the planet Saturn, the planet would float. Saturn is less dense than water!
- There is a type of jellyfish, called *Turritopsis dohrnii,* that can age in reverse. This jellyfish can get younger and younger until its life cycle starts again—enabling the jellyfish to live forever!
- Folding a piece of paper in half doubles its thickness. If you were able to fold it in half forty-five times, it would be tall enough to reach the moon!

Now, after reading those facts and thinking about them, tell us a little bit about how it makes you feel:

_____

_____

_____

Bigger Than Us

There you have it. Each pillar of Meaning asks us to view our lives from outside ourselves, or outside a single moment. Each pillar asks you to shrink down, make yourself and your own experience smaller, and take a look at the big picture.

This brings us back around to that shrinking ant guy again. As a superhero, he finds he has the most impact when he's super tiny, almost undetectable to the human eye. He's not the center of attention, but he's powerful and changes the course of battles for the better. When we think about Meaning, it's not always easy to remember each of the four pillars, but we always remember that ant guy. Meaning is about being a powerful part of something much bigger than any of us could ever be on our own. When we think like that ant guy, suddenly we feel **Energized** again.

Try this exercise!

Ask "Why?" Remember all the way back to chapter 8, when we were talking about "Why?" We asked "Why do we do homework?" and "Why do we need to go to college?" We had some pretty simple answers at the time, and each answer was related to a destination on our Good-Life Maps. The thing is, if you keep asking "Why," it can be a powerful tool that can help you drill down to the real motivation for doing something.

Think of something you do each week or every day and ask yourself why you do it. Once you get an answer, question that answer by asking "Why?" again. Then again. Maybe even again! You are going to ask "Why?" at least three to five times before you get to the real reason or motivation for doing something.

Example:

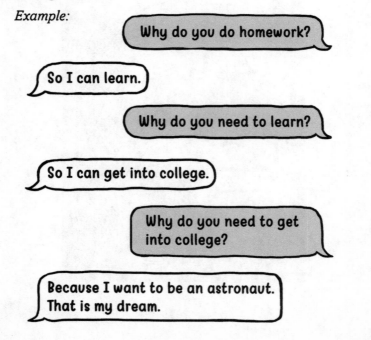

Why do you do homework?

So I can learn.

Why do you need to learn?

So I can get into college.

Why do you need to get into college?

Because I want to be an astronaut. That is my dream.

Your turn:

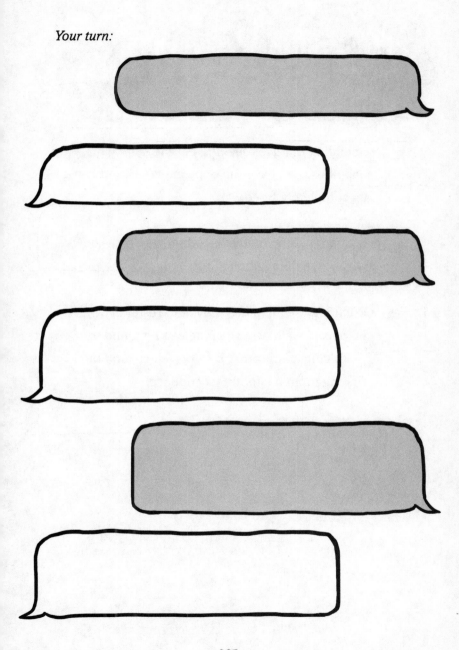

- Spending our lives seeking out the feeling of happiness can have the opposite effect and leave us completely Fried.

- It's hard to stay motivated when we don't know why we're doing something.

- Pursuing Meaning has proven to result in increased wellness. Meaning can be found in Belonging, in purpose, by storytelling, and by finding moments of transcendence.

CHAPTER 14
RESILIENT

Jasmin stared out the window of the bus. She was trying desper-
ately to avoid looking at the crumpled paper in her hand for the
thousandth time. Eventually, she couldn't help herself and glanced
again, hoping to see something different. Nope. The same bright red
letter D at the top of her essay. Her heart ached. She'd worked so
hard on this assignment. "Why me? This is the worst thing that's
ever happened to me," she sighed.

Suddenly she was jolted by a not-so-gentle punch on the shoul-
der. "Ahh!" she yelped as Judy, her twin sister, slid into the seat next
to her.

Judy saw Jasmin's paper and screeched, "NO WAY! Wonder
twins activate in the form of almost failing grades!" Judy lifted up
her paper and revealed the same D on top of the same exact assign-
ment. "I didn't have time to show you before gym started!" Judy
said, and chuckled.

"Judes, we both got Ds on the history essay. You can't seriously
think this is funny."

"Well, not funny, but, like, not the end of the world, either. I

mean, I felt bad about it all through gym, but then I thought, Well,
I'll just try harder next time. Right?"

"Whatever."

"Hey! Since we're identical, do you think if only one of us stud-
ies next time, the other will get a better grade, too?"

"Stop joking around, Judes! You don't get it, do you? There isn't
gonna be a next time. I'm never trying again. What's the point? I'm
just not smart."

Throughout part three of this book, we've told you about the
different fuels to boost your superpowers, but we have a feeling that this one might be your favorite. The fuel for the superpower of being Resilient will take you well beyond fixing
what's going wrong, to living an awesome superpowered life!
So, what are you waiting for? Oh, you're waiting for us. . . .
Sorry! Here you go!

In the story above, Jasmin and Judy face the same challenge: a bad grade. Yet they have totally different reactions.
Jasmin falls into a negative spiral and decides she's giving up.
Judy bounces back and says the grade made her feel bad, but
she's going to try harder next time. The main question is *why?*
Why did two people facing the same challenge have totally
different reactions?

When we present this story and ask this question to grown-
ups and kids alike, we hear some common theories about why
Judy and Jasmin have different reactions:

Maybe it's the way they were raised.

Not a bad guess, but in this case, Jasmin and Judy were raised by the same parents.

Maybe it's their genes.

Again, a good thought, but Jasmin and Judy are identical twins and so their genes and biology are almost exactly the same.

Maybe it's their environment.

Jasmin and Judy grew up in the same home, eating nearly the same foods, and spending time in the same environments.

Maybe one of them just had more challenges growing up or a harder childhood.

Could be, but as you'll find out, it's not the big reason why their reactions were different.

It would seem that since they were raised by the same parents in the same home and have close-to-identical DNA, they should react nearly the same way, right? Eh. Not so much. Science shows us that the biggest thing affecting your

Resilience, or your ability to bounce back after a challenge, is *not* your genes, environment, opportunities, wealth, or childhood experiences. **The biggest thing that affects how you react to a challenge is *not* the challenge itself; it's the way you *think* about the challenge.**

Do you get the AWESOMENESS of what we just said?!

It's not the big speech coming up. . . . It's *the way you think* about the big speech.

It's not the birthday party where you have to socialize. . . . It's *the way you think* about the birthday party where you have to socialize.

It's not the person you want to make friends with. . . . It's *the way you think* about the person you want to make friends with.

It's not the challenge itself. . . . It's *the way you think* about the challenge that affects your ability to be **Resilient**!

So, while you can't control who your parents are, your genes, or the challenges that come your way, you do have control over *the way you think* about something. You can make a choice about your attitude, or what is called your mindset. Your mindset is the way you look at the world, and it's the secret fuel that activates your superpower of being **Resilient.**

Mindset → Resilience

We've touched on mindsets throughout this book, but it's time to really dive deep into three different mindsets of super-powered kids!

#1: Hope

In the story of Jasmin and Judy above, Judy was able to look on the bright side of things and feel hopeful about the future. Jasmin believed it was the worst challenge she'd ever faced and didn't feel hopeful about the future. Judy had more of what researchers call an optimistic mindset, while Jasmin had a pessimistic mindset.

> **Optimistic mindset** = looking at the bright side of things, feeling hopeful about a situation

> **Pessimistic mindset** = thinking about the negative or worst things, not feeling hope about a situation

Your genes, and other things that are out of your control, do play a role in whether you're more of an optimist or a pessimist. However, we're here to talk about what you can control . . . the way you explain the good or bad stuff in your life. Scientists call this an explanatory style. When it comes to challenges, an optimist's and a pessimist's explanatory style is different in three clear ways. Circle which style you usually use:

1. How long will the challenge last?

- Pessimists think bad things last forever (permanent).
- Optimists think bad things come to an end (temporary).

2. What part of your life is affected?

- Pessimists think a challenge in one part of life affects every part of life (pervasive).
- Optimists think a challenge in one part of life affects one part of life (specific).

3. Who's to blame for this challenge?

- Pessimists blame themselves for challenges (personalize).
- Optimists look for all the reasons for challenges (externalize).

So, how do you think about your challenges? More like a pessimist, where challenges last forever, affect all parts of your life, and they're all your fault? Or more like an optimist, where challenges have an end, affect one part of your life, and are caused by something outside yourself?

It turns out, whatever you circled above doesn't matter.

Well, what we mean is, no matter how you're wired at this moment, you can change your style. You can choose to use an optimistic explanatory style, and with practice, your hope mindset can change. Changing your explanatory style can take you . . .

From:

"I'm never going to make friends at this new school."

To:

"I don't have friends at this new school,
but it won't always be like this."

From:

"I feel anxious. My life and everything in it sucks."

To:

"Feeling anxious is hard, but there are lots
of amazing parts of my life."

From:

"I wish I'd made the volleyball team.
This is all my fault."

To:

"There were kids who have been playing
volleyball for years. It was competitive."

How about you try changing some thoughts of your own? To make it easier for you, we've built you a Hope Machine! No need to thank us; it was our pleasure!

Flip the page and check out how pessimistic statements go into the Hope Machine and come out transformed into optimistic ones. We've left you room to try out the machine yourself!

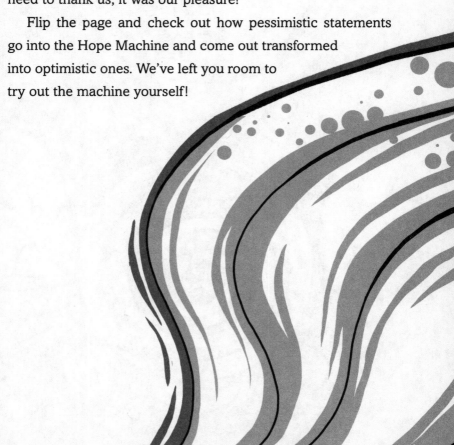

#2: Courage

"You're so smart!"

You've probably been hearing some version of this line from the moment you were born! We're all a little obsessed with how smart we are, or how smart other people think we are. Don't get us wrong; it's wonderful to have a great mind. We're not saying you shouldn't take pride in this, but what we want to talk about is your mindset, or your belief about how intelligence works. Time for a one-question quiz:

---

1. My intelligence can change with effort and hard work. TRUE or FALSE

You probably want us to give you the answer, and we will, but first we need to tell you something even more interesting than the answer.

About thirty years ago, a few scientists studied how students handled failure. They learned that some students bounce back after failing and others don't, even when the setback is small. These researchers wanted to know why. Ultimately, they realized the key was mindset. It wasn't about students being able to improve their intelligence through effort and hard work. It was about students *believing* their intelligence could change. That's what made all the difference. It turns out there are two main mindsets when it comes to intelligence:

> **Growth mindset:** You believe how smart you are **can** change.

> **Fixed mindset:** You believe how smart you are **cannot** change.

Thinking again about our "wonder twins," Jasmin said she wasn't going to try harder, because she believed "I'm just not smart." She didn't think her effort mattered. It sounds like Jasmin thinks how smart she is will never change. She has a fixed mindset. Judy doesn't think that one test score defines her. Judy believes she can get smarter with hard work and effort. Judy has a growth mindset. These two different mindsets affect behavior in many ways. Here are three of the main differences:

1. Making an Effort

- Fixed mindset students think that if they have to put in effort for something, they're obviously not good at that thing. They don't try as hard.
- Growth mindset students think success comes from making an effort. They try hard.

2. Challenges

- Fixed mindset students give up when they're challenged.
- Growth mindset students keep going when they're challenged.

3. Mistakes

- Fixed mindset students don't like to appear "not smart," and so they hide mistakes or just take fewer risks.
- Growth mindset students know that mistakes are an important part of learning and take more risks.

Now, if you have a fixed mindset and think you're just stuck with the smarts you have, don't feel bad. A lot of us think that way, or have in the past (including us)! The amazing thing is that if you have a fixed mindset, it's not really fixed; you can *change* your mindset. The first step in changing your mindset is to understand that we're not asking you to just believe in a myth. Your intelligence actually *can* change with hard work and effort, because brains are plastic!

We don't mean your brain is made of the same stuff as water bottles. . . . We're talking about the fact that your brain can change and be shaped based on your experiences. This ability is called neuroplasticity. It even happens when you make mistakes!

While your brain is an organ, it acts a lot like a muscle. Weight lifting breaks down muscles by creating tiny little tears in the muscle, until eventually the muscle repairs itself and gets bigger and stronger. When you make mistakes, synapses (parts of your brain that are active when you're learning) fire, and the brain actually physically changes and grows. In the end, mistakes aren't just opportunities to learn; the struggle actually makes your brain stronger.

Okay, ready to try another machine? We like to call this the Courage Machine (for obvious reasons, we think)! It helps you go from a fixed mindset to a growth mindset by changing your language. You will go . . .

From: "

I guess I'm just not that smart."

To:

"I guess I haven't learned that yet."

From:

"I hope I'm the best on the team!"

To:

"I hope there are people on the team who challenge me."

From:

"I lost. Maybe I'm not as good as I thought."

To: "

I lost. Maybe I can learn something from the winner."

Turn the page to see the machine and write in your own statements!

#3: Motivation

You might have picked up this book thinking you wanted to stress and worry less. Hopefully, we've made it clear throughout the book that getting rid of stress and worry would be like getting rid of part of who you are as a human. Instead of trying to stress less, the goal is for you to *stress better*. Part of stressing better means choosing the right stress mindset. Which one of these two describes your mindset when it comes to stress?

Stress is harmful: Stress makes me less healthy, makes me less motivated, and makes me do worse in school. Stress is basically a bad thing that I should try to avoid.

Stress is helpful: Stress can boost my health, motivate me, and help me do better in school. Stress is basically a positive experience in life.

Most people have the first mindset, that stress is harmful. You might even think it's weird to view stress as helpful. In fact, when we bring this idea up, sometimes kids and adults wonder if the people with the "stress is helpful" mindset actually have any *real* stress in their lives. Of course they do. People with a more positive view of stress actually face real challenges and struggles. They just happen to believe that stress isn't *all* bad. It turns out that the science supports this belief.

You may have heard that "stress hormones," or chemicals that release in your body when you're stressed, can damage your body. What you don't hear about is how in many stressful situations, the stress hormones released in your body help you. It turns out that stress hormones can boost your motivation, productivity, creativity, courage, and social connection; can improve learning and growth in your brain; and can even strengthen your heart!

The way you view stress changes how you behave, in a few ways:

1. Facing problems
- "Stress is harmful" mindsets focus on getting rid of feelings.
- "Stress is helpful" mindsets focus on facing and solving problems.

2. Being productive
- "Stress is harmful" mindsets can cause you to feel more fatigued and make you less productive.
- "Stress is helpful" mindsets can give you more energy and make you more productive.

3. Reaching goals
- People with "stress is harmful" mindsets get overwhelmed and stop pursuing goals that cause too much stress.
- People with "stress is helpful" mindsets see stress as a challenge and keep going toward goals.

You can start using stress to help you get motivated and more productive right now! Before big games, athletes often feel stress, but they might talk about being "pumped up" or "amped" or "excited." These words help transform their stress into motivation. Time for you to use stress to get motivated. Yes, you've guessed right. We've built one final machine for you—the Motivation Machine. Put in your stressful thoughts, and they will transform into excitement. The machine is already hard at work, changing statements:

From:
"I wish I could just calm down before this speech!"
To:
"I'm excited about this speech!"

From:

*"If I can't calm down before
the game, I'll blow it!"*

To:

*"I can use this excitement to give
me strength and focus."*

From:

*"I'm so nervous. I have butterflies
in my stomach!"*

To:

*"All these butterflies in my stomach
are going to help me do well."*

Now you try! Turn the page and fire up
the Motivation Machine!

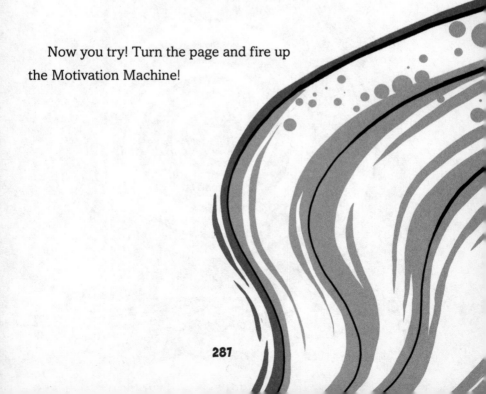

Try these exercises!

1. Fill in the mindset. You've learned that when we struggle, it's not always the challenge that we need to

1. Challenge

1. Challenge

2. Hope

2. Courage

3. Reaction

3. Reaction

change but the way we think about the challenge. Help these kids change the way they think about their challenges. Give them hope, courage, and motivation!

1. Challenge

1. Challenge

2. Motivation

2. Motivation

3. Reaction

3. Reaction

2. **Growth or fixed?** If you have a growth mindset, you believe your intelligence can change with hard work and effort. If you have a fixed mindset, you believe the intelligence you were born with doesn't change with hard work and effort. You can hear the two different mindsets in the statements below. Draw an arrow from the different statements to the right mindset area.

Challenges make my brain stronger.

I know my brain is making connections when I struggle.

It's not worth trying. I'm not good at it.

I believe I can get better through hard work and effort.

I like challenges.

When I try hard things, my brain grows.

Mistakes help me learn.

GROWTH

How sma I am and how good am at thir will neve change.

FIXED

I listen to feedback from others.

I'm not good at this subject—I was just born this way.

Failing at something is a huge waste of time.

I try difficult things.

3. **Design a mindset poster!** Imagine you are running for student council president and your campaign is all about helping students develop hope, courage, and motivation mindsets. What would your campaign slogan be? What would your poster look like? Sample posters are on the following pages! Time to create your own poster!

(Answers: Growth statements are "Challenges make my brain stronger." "I know my brain is making connections when I struggle." "I like challenges." "When I try hard things, my brain grows." "Mistakes help me learn." "I listen to feedback from others." "I try difficult things." Fixed statements are "It's not worth trying. I'm not good at it." "I'm not good at this subject—I was just born this way." "Failing at something is a huge waste of time.")

MINDSET
#superpowered
FAILING IS A CHANCE TO GROW
i'm PERFECT, IMPERFECT
BRING 'EM ON!
CHALLENGES?

MINDSET #superpowered

MISTAKES HELP MY

BRAIN

G R O W

i take itty-bitty steps to reach big goals

GOOD ENOUGH is awesome

i ♥ feedback — it makes me better

EVERYTHING

I CAN LIVE WITHOUT THESE WORDS

ALWAYS

NOTHING

MINDSET #superpowered

- Your ability to bounce back from a challenge has less to do with the actual challenge and more to do with the way you think about it, or your mindset.

- You have a choice when it comes to your mindset. One of the most powerful ways to shift mindsets is to change the way you talk to yourself.

- Three mindsets that boost being **Resilient** are optimistic, growth, and stress-is-helpful, all of which increase your hope, courage, and motivation.

CROSSING THE FINISH LINE

Here we are. The end. We asked you to trust us, and you did. We're sure it wasn't always easy for you, but you stuck with us and pushed through, and we're so happy that you're here, at the finish line!

You've learned how to turn your time-traveling, What-iffing thoughts into more Mindful, **Present** observations. You've changed your old Camouflaged, people-pleasing self into a mold-breaking **Original.** Remember when you were Cocooned? Well, now you have the tools to curb those perfectionistic habits, to feel **Whole** and have a strong sense of belonging. And doesn't it feel good to go from feeling Fried to walking on an **Energized** path toward a totally Meaningful life? Let's not forget being Iced with paralyzing fear. That was no fun, was it? Well, just be proud of the fact that you know how to change your mindset and you're ready to show off your power of being **Resilient.**

Yup! The POWER is now yours!

If you just read that summary and felt like there was something majorly wrong with it, then you're onto us. It's only fitting that we wrap up this book with one more giant truth: there is no finish line. Don't get us wrong. You are now superpowered, and you have the tools and knowledge to overcome many of life's obstacles, but just like you never stop exercising if you want to keep your body healthy, we hope you never stop exercising your superpowers. You'll face more challenges. You'll need to be reminded of the strengths you naturally carry inside you. When that happens, return to these pages. Do the activities over again. Being superpowered is a process, a journey, not a destination.

Now, we once heard somewhere (we're not sure where) that with great power comes great responsibility. You, of course, have great POWER. You are **Present, Original, Whole, Energized,** and **Resilient**! And while it was our responsibility to help you rediscover what has always been within you, it is now your responsibility, if you choose to accept it, to do your best to live each day superpowered. Life might not always look perfect, but you should know by now that it doesn't have to be. Practice your skills, and you will go beyond surviving the challenges, into living each day thriving with joy and Meaning. The best part? When you live a superpowered life, you inevitably inspire others to reactivate their own superpowers, and they inspire others, and so on. Together, we can change the world. ♥

Certificate of Awesome!

This is to certify that _____ has completed
the Superpowered Program, and, most importantly, has
learned _____
_____, and from this point forward, will
_____
_____

Witnesses

Renee Jain
Dr. _____

SUPERPOWERED
SP
SEAL OF AUTHENTICITY

MY SUPERPOWERED SELF

NOTES

Chapter 4: The Messenger

45 Millions of people feel just like you:

American Psychological Association. (2018). *Stress in America: Generation Z*. Stress in America™ Survey.

American Psychological Association. (2017). *Stress in America: The state of our nation*. Stress in America™ Survey.

Baxter, A., Scott, K., Vos, T., & Whiteford, H. (2013). Global prevalence of anxiety disorders: A systematic review and meta-regression. *Psychological Medicine, 43*(5), 897–910. doi:10.1017/S003329171200147X

Child Mind Institute. (2015). *Children's mental health report*. New York.

45 Worry has benefits:

American Psychological Association. (2019, August 10). Why stress and anxiety aren't always bad: Expecting to always feel happy and relaxed a recipe for disappointment. *ScienceDaily.*

McGonigal, K. (2016). *The upside of stress: Why stress is good for you, and how to get good at it*. New York, NY: Avery.

46 fight, flight, or freeze response:

Cannon, W. B. (1915). *Bodily changes in pain, hunger, fear and rage: An account of recent researches into the function of emotional excitement*. New York, NY: D. Appleton. doi:10.1037/10013-000

46 you don't necessarily go into fight, flight, or freeze:

Kemeny, M. E. (2003). The psychobiology of stress. *Current Directions in Psychological Science, 12*(4), 124–129. doi:10.1111/1467-8721.01246

48 it's the way we *think* about the feeling:

Crum, A. J., Salovey, P., & Achor, S. (2013). Rethinking stress: The role of mindsets in determining the stress response. *Journal of Personality and Social Psychology, 104*(4), 716–733. doi:10.1037/a0031201

Keller, A., Litzelman, K., Wisk, L. E., Maddox, T., Cheng, E. R., Creswell, P. D., & Witt, W. P. (2012). Does the perception that stress affects health matter? The association with health and mortality. *Health Psychology: Official Journal of the Division of Health Psychology, American Psychological Association, 31*(5), 677–684. doi:10.1037/a0026743

57 Message Type #1: Blaze:

Jansen, A. S. P., Nguyen, X. V., Karpitskiy, V., Mettenleiter, T. C., & Loewy, A. D. (1995). Central command neurons of the sympathetic nervous system: Basis of the fight-or-flight response. *Science, 270*(5236), 644–646. doi:10.1126/science.270.5236.644

58 Message Type #2: Challenge:

Seery, M. D. (2013). The biopsychosocial model of challenge and threat: Using the heart to measure the mind. *Social and Personality Psychology Compass, 7*(9), 637–653. doi:10.1111/spc3.12052

58 Jump from worry to excitement:

Brooks, A. W. (2014). Get excited: Reappraising pre-performance anxiety as excitement with minimal cues. *PsycEXTRA Dataset. doi:10.1037/e578192014-321*

59 Message Type #3: Connect:

Taylor, S. E., Klein, L. C., Lewis, B. P., Gruenewald, T. L., Gurung, R. A. R., & Updegraff, J. A. (2000). Biobehavioral responses to stress in females: Tend-and-befriend, not fight-or-flight. *Psychological Review, 107*(3), 411–429. doi:10.1037//0033 -295x.107.3.411

60 Message Type #4: Spam:

Clark, D. A. (2005). *Intrusive thoughts in clinical disorders: Theory, research, and treatment.* New York, NY: Guilford Press.

Chapter 5: What-iffing

66 At any moment we can drive forward into the future:

Johnson, S. (2018, November 18). The human brain is a time traveler. *New York Times Magazine.* Retrieved from nytimes.com /interactive/2018/11/15/magazine/tech -design-ai-prediction.html

66 nearly half our time:

Killingsworth, M. A., & Gilbert, D. T. (2010). A wandering mind is an unhappy mind. *Science, 330*(6006), 932. doi:10.1126 /science.1192439

72 Humans are typically considered:

Seligman, M. E. P. (2016). *Homo prospectus.* Oxford: Oxford University Press.

72 It has a simulation feature:

Beck, J. (2017, October 17). Imagining the future is just another form of memory. *Atlantic.* Retrieved from theatlantic.com /science/archive/2017/10/imagining -the-future-is-just-another-form-of -memory/542832

Eagleman, D. (2017). *The brain: The story of you.* New York, NY: Vintage Books.

72 harder for the logical part:

Park, J., Wood, J., Bondi, C., Arco, A. D., & Moghaddam, B. (2016). Anxiety evokes hypofrontality and disrupts rule-relevant encoding by dorsomedial prefrontal cortex neurons. *Journal of Neuroscience, 36*(11), 3322–3335. doi:10.1523 /jneurosci.4250-15.2016

73 scientists call this thought suppression:

Wegner, D. M. (1994). Ironic processes of mental control. *Psychological Review, 101*(1), 34–52. doi:10.1037//0033 -295x.101.1.34;

Wegner, D. M., Schneider, D. J., Carter, S. R., & White, T. L. (1987). Paradoxical effects of thought suppression. *Journal of Personality and Social Psychology, 53*(1), 5–13. doi:10.1037//0022-3514.53.1.5

75 Getting mad at yourself:

Warren, R., Smeets, E., & Neff, K. D. (2016). Self-criticism and self-compassion: Risk and resilience for psychopathology. *Current Psychiatry, 15*(12), 18–32.

76 What-iffing dominoes:

Gellatly, R., & Beck, A. T. (2016). Catastrophic thinking: A transdiagnostic process across psychiatric disorders. *Cognitive Therapy and Research, 40*(4), 441–452. doi:10.1007 /s10608-016-9763-3

78 if-then plans:

Gollwitzer, P. M. (1999). Implementation intentions: Strong effects of simple plans. *American Psychologist, 54*(7), 493–503. doi:10.1037/0003-066x.54.7.493

Chapter 6: Camouflaged

85 when a person feels left out:

Kross, E., Berman, M. G., Mischel, W., Smith, E. E., & Wager, T. D. (2011). Social rejection shares somatosensory representations with physical pain. *Proceedings of the National Academy of Sciences, 108*(15), 6270–6275. doi:10.1073/pnas.1102693108

85 Social anxiety:

Child Mind Institute. (2019). Social anxiety disorder basics. Retrieved from childmind. org/guide/social-anxiety-disorder/#social -anxiety-what-is-it

87 your thoughts, your feelings, and your actions:

Ellis, A. (1999). *Reason and emotion in psychotherapy: A comprehensive method of treating human disturbances.* New York, NY: Citadel.

89 they contain errors or mistakes:

Beck, A. T. (1979). *Cognitive therapy and the emotional disorders.* New York, NY: New American Library.

Burns, D. D. (2009). *Feeling good: The new mood therapy.* New York: Harper.

89 eleven million pieces of information:

Zimmermann, M. (1986). Neurophysiology of sensory systems. *Fundamentals of Sensory Physiology*, 68–116. doi:10.1007/978-3-642-82598-9_3

89 Your brain needs to filter out information:

Nørretranders, T., & Sydenham, J. (1999). *The user illusion: Cutting consciousness down to size.* New York, NY: Penguin Putnam.

102 Laddering:

Abramowitz, J. S., Deacon, B. J., & Whiteside, S. P. H. (2019). *Exposure therapy for anxiety* (2nd ed.) New York, NY: Guilford.

Chapter 7: Cocooned

109 Perfectionism is about hiding our imperfections:

Brown, B. (2010). *The gifts of imperfection: Let go of who you think you're supposed to be and embrace who you are.* Center City, MN: Hazelden.

Santanello, A. W., & Gardner, F. L. (2006). The role of experiential avoidance in the relationship between maladaptive perfectionism and worry. *Cognitive Therapy and Research, 31*(3), 319–332. doi:10.1007/s10608-006-9000-6

121 WOOP:

Oettingen, G. (2015). *Rethinking positive thinking.* New York, NY: Current.

125 big goals into smaller goals:

Pychyl, T. A. (2013). *Solving the procrastination puzzle: A concise guide to strategies for change.* New York: Jeremy P. Tarcher/Penguin.

127 taking action is twice as effective:

Neal, D. T., Wood, W., & Quinn, J. M. (2006). Habits—A repeat performance. *Current Corrections in Psychological Science, 15*(4), 198–202. doi:10.1111/j.1467 -8721.2006.00435.x

128 harder for you to reach your goals:

Neff, K. (2015). *Self-compassion: The proven power of being kind to yourself.* New York, NY: William Morrow.

Chapter 8: Fried

138 The Problem with Happiness:

Brocas, I., & Carrillo, J. D. (2004). *The psychology of economic decisions.* Oxford: Oxford University Press.

Mauss, I. B., Tamir, M., Anderson, C. L., & Savino, N. S. (2011). Can seeking happiness make people unhappy? Paradoxical effects of valuing happiness. *Emotion, 11*(4), 807–815. doi:10.1037/a0022010

139 All feelings have value:

Ekman, P. (2007). *Emotions revealed: Recognizing faces and feelings to improve communication and emotional life.* New York, NY: St. Martins Griffin.

141 Here are some of the things they found:

Buettner, D. (2012). *The blue zones: 9 lessons for living longer from the people who've lived the longest.* Washington, DC: National Geographic.

144 Motivation is an inside job:

Ryan, R. M., & Deci, E. L. (2018). *Self-determination theory: Basic psychological needs in motivation, development, and wellness.* New York, NY: Guilford Press.

147 Flow:

Csikszentmihalyi, M. (2009). *Flow: The psychology of optimal experience.* New York, NY: Harper Row.

Chapter 9: Iced

158 What are panic attacks?:

Anxiety and Depression Association of America. (2018). Understand the facts: Symptoms. Retrieved from adaa.org /understanding-anxiety/panic-disorder -agoraphobia/symptoms

158 make panic worse:

Clark, D. M. (1986). A cognitive approach to panic. *Behaviour Research and Therapy, 24*(4), 461–470.

Hayes, S. C., Wilson, K. G., Gifford, E. V., Follette, V. M., & Al, E. (1996). Experiential avoidance and behavioral disorders: A functional dimensional approach to diagnosis and treatment. *Journal of Consulting and Clinical Psychology, 64*(6), 1152–1168. doi:10.1037//0022-006x.64.6.1152

Pauli, P., Marquardt, C., Hartl, L., Nutzinger, D. O., Hölzl, R., & Strian, F. (1991). Anxiety induced by cardiac perceptions in patients with panic attacks: A field study. *Behaviour Research and Therapy, 29*(2), 137–145. doi:10.1016/0005-7967(91)90042-2

159 a huge discovery:

LeDoux, J. E. (2016). *Anxious: Using the brain to understand and treat fear and anxiety.* New York, NY: Penguin Books.

LeDoux, J. E. (2015, August 15). The amygdala is NOT the brain's fear center. *Psychology Today.* Retrieved from psychologytoday .com/us/blog/i-got-mind-tell-you/201508 /the-amygdala-is-not-the-brains-fear -center

163 change your performance:

Jamieson, J. P., Mendes, W. B., Blackstock, E., & Schmader, T. (2010). Turning the knots in your stomach into bows: Reappraising arousal improves performance on the GRE. *Journal of Experimental Social Psychology, 46*(1), 208–212. doi:10.1016 /j.jesp.2009.08.015

Jamieson, J. P., Peters, B. J., Greenwood, E. J., & Altose, A. J. (2016). Reappraising stress arousal improves performance and reduces evaluation anxiety in classroom exam situations. *Social Psychological and Personality Science, 7*(6), 579–587. doi:10.1177/1948550616644656

Chapter 10: Present

180 cognitive fusion:

Harris, R. (2019). *ACT made simple: An easy-to-read primer on acceptance and commitment therapy.* Oakland, CA: New Harbinger Publications, Inc.

185 sing it:

Harris, R. (2011). Mindfulness without meditation. *Healthcare Counseling and Psychotherapy Journal, 9*(4), 21–24.

Chapter 11: Original

193 "as poor as it is possible to be . . .":

Rowling, J. K. (2008, June 5). Text of J. K. Rowling's speech. *Harvard Gazette*.

198 the heart is amazing:

(2017.) *Heart Intelligence: Connecting with the Intuitive Guidance of the Heart*. Waterfront Digital Press.

201 Inner Voices in Action:

Anti-Bullying Crusader. (n.d.). Anti-bullying day: May 4. Retrieved from antibullyingcrusader.com/day/anti-bullying-day

CBC News. (2017, September 17). Bullied student tickled pink by schoolmates' t-shirt campaign. CBC/Radio-Canada. Retrieved from cbc.ca/news/canada/bullied-student-tickled-pink-by-schoolmates-t-shirt-campaign-1.682221

206 Step #2: Argue More:

Grant, A. (2017, November 4). Kids, would you please start fighting? *New York Times*. Retrieved from nytimes.com/2017/11/04/opinion/sunday/kids-would-you-please-start-fighting.html

209 "I didn't fit in in high school . . ." through ". . . doesn't mean you're not a winner":

Lady Gaga. (2011, January 11). Lady Gaga shares everything [Video file]. *TheEllenShow*. Retrieved from youtube.com/watch?v=NOpSC9F04IU

209 "It is your right to choose . . ." through ". . . I know that person":

Lady Gaga. (2015, October 24). Emotion revolution closing session [Video file]. *Yale University*. Retrieved from youtube.com/watch?time_continue=10&v=P5Xus-Y0biQ

Chapter 12: Whole

219 Fitting in is about changing yourself:

Brown, B. (2019). *Braving the wilderness: The quest for true belonging and the courage to stand alone*. New York: Random House.

221 a small town . . . called Roseto:

Bruhn, J. G., & Wolf, S. (2003). *The Roseto story: An anatomy of health*. Norman, OK: University of Oklahoma Press.

Egolf, B., Lasker, J., Wolf, S., & Potvin, L. (1992). The Roseto effect: A 50-year comparison of mortality rates. *American Journal of Public Health, 82*(8), 1089–1092. doi:10.2105/ajph.82.8.1089

223 People who overthink often have great imaginations:

Perkins, A. M., Arnone, D., Smallwood, J., & Mobbs, D. (2015). Thinking too much: Self-generated thought as the engine of neuroticism. *Trends in Cognitive Sciences, 19*(9), 492–498. doi:10.1016/j.tics.2015.07.003

223 When you are sensitive to your own emotions:

Aron, E. (2002). *The highly sensitive child: Helping our children thrive when the world overwhelms them*. New York: Harmony Books.

224 You may feel overwhelmed or tired at a big, noisy party:

Cain, S. (2013). *Quiet: The power of introverts in a world that can't stop talking*. New York: Broadway Books.

224 a characteristic of a great leader:

Trapp, R. (2015, January 30). Anxious leaders make better decisions. *Forbes*.

226 Solomon Asch conducted a now-famous experiment:

Asch, S.E. (1955). Opinions and social pressure. *Scientific American, 193*(5), 31–35.

Asch, S.E. (1956). Studies of independence and conformity: A minority of one against a unanimous majority. *Psychological Monographs, 70*(9), 1–70. doi:10.1037/h0093718

228 Jackie Robinson:

Biography.com Editors. (2019, August 28). Jackie Robinson biography, *Biography.com, A&E Television Networks*. Retrieved from biography.com/athlete/jackie-robinson

233 Strengths Tree:

Peterson, C., & Seligman, M. E. P. (2004). *Character strengths and virtues: A handbook and classification*. New York: Oxford University Press.

242 Loving-kindness:

Fredrickson, B. L., Cohn, M. A., Coffey, K. A., Pek, J., & Finkel, S. M. (2008). Open hearts build lives: Positive emotions, induced through loving-kindness meditation, build consequential personal resources. *Journal of Personality and Social Psychology, 95*(5), 1045–1062. doi:10.1037/a0013262

Kok, B. E., Coffey, K. A., Cohn, M. A., Catalino, L. I., Vacharkulksemsuk, T., Algoe, S. B., & Fredrickson, B. L. (2013). How positive emotions build physical health: Perceived positive social connections account for the upward spiral between positive emotions and vagal tone. *Psychological Science, 24*(7), 1123–1132 doi:10.1177/0956797612470827

Chapter 13: Energized

249 four pillars of meaning:

Smith, E. E. (2017). *The power of meaning: Finding fulfillment in a world obsessed with happiness*. New York: Broadway Books.

262 fit the planet Saturn:

Nasa.gov. Extreme space facts. Nasa.gov. Retrieved from jpl.nasa.gov/edu/pdfs /ss_extreme_poster.pdf

262 type of jellyfish called *Turritopsis dohrn*:

Lisenkova, A. P., Grigorenko, T. V., Tyazhelova, T. V., Andreeva, F. E., Gusev, A. D., Manakhov, A., . . . Rogaev, E. I. Complete mitochondrial genome and evolutionary analysis of *turritopsis dohrnii*, the "immortal" jellyfish with a reversible life-cycle. *Molecular Phylogenetics and Evolution, 107*(2017), 232–238. doi:10.1016 /j.ympev.2016.11.007

262 Folding a piece of paper in half:

Paenza, Adrian. (n.d.). How folding paper can get you to the moon. *TED-Ed*. Retrieved from ed.ted.com/lessons/how-folding -paper-can-get-you-to-the-moon

Chapter 14: Resilient

271 The biggest thing that affects how you react:

Reivich, K., & Shatté, A. (2003). *The resilience factor: 7 essential skills for overcoming life's inevitable obstacles*. New York: Harmony Books.

272 optimistic mindset; pessimistic mindset; explanatory style:

Abramson, L. Y., Seligman, M. E., & Teasdale, J. D. (1978). Learned helplessness in humans: Critique and reformulation. *Journal of Abnormal Psychology, 87*(1), 49–74. doi:10.1037//0021-843x.87.1.49

Seligman, M. E. P. (2011). *Learned optimism: How to change your mind and life*. New York: Vintage.

279 growth mindset; fixed mindset:

Dweck, C. S. (2007). *Mindset: The new psychology of success*. New York: Ballantine Books.

281 Taxi drivers in London:

Woollett, K., & Maguire, E. A. (2011). Acquiring "the knowledge" of London's layout drives structural brain changes. *Current Biology, 21*(24), 2109–2114. doi:10.1016 /j.cub.2011.11.018

284 stress mindset:

McGonigal, K. (2016). *The upside of stress: Why stress is good for you, and how to get good at it*. New York: Avery.

GLOSSARY

3Fs: three natural ways the body responds when under immediate stress or danger—fight, flight, or freeze

5Cs: a five-step process for fixing a "ThoughtHole," or a thinking mistake—catch, check, collect, challenge, change

anxiety: as defined in *Superpowered:* constantly worrying, or feeling nervous and uneasy about everyday things like school, next week's soccer game, not being liked, something uncertain, or an upcoming event; or even worrying about worrying

Belonging: accepting yourself for who you truly are (including your quirky traits, too), and feeling a sense of friendship and community within a larger unit of people, as opposed to changing who you are to "fit in" with groups; Belonging is the fuel for your superpower of being Whole

Blaze message: you get this message in real dangerous situations, such as fires, getting lost, or getting hurt; Blaze messages activate the 3Fs!

Camouflaged: when you've changed or hidden parts of yourself in order to fit in socially; this happens when your superpower of being Original has been zapped

Challenge message: you get this message in situations like taking a test, making a speech, performing, or being at social events; Challenge messages want to provide you with motivation, focus, and energy during challenges

Cocooned: when you've hidden who you truly are, as a form of self-protection; you may Cocoon when you're afraid of making a mistake, or when you hold the incorrect belief that who you are is based on things such as your grades, your looks, your "likes" on social media, etc.; this happens when your superpower of being Whole has been zapped

Connect message: you get this message when you feel overwhelmed or when your feelings have been badly hurt; Connect messages tell us we need support from a close family member or friend

distraction: when you try to distract yourself from uncomfortable feelings (Example: "Something is wrong. I just need to watch TV, eat, and pretend like it's not happening." See "Panic Made Worse" illustration.)

Extremifying: a thinking mistake (a ThoughtHole); viewing situations in extremes, using terms like "always" or "never" or "the worst"

faulty connections: avoiding people, places, or things that you think are connected to your panic (Example: "I had that panic attack because I went to the grocery store. I am never going there again." See "Panic Made Worse" illustration.)

"feel like" statements: you feel like something more than panic or anxiety is happening to your body. (Example: "I feel like something is terribly wrong with my body." See "Panic Made Worse" illustration.)

flip the switch: get inspired by others rather than feeling envious of them

flow: a state of being where you are focused and engaged in an activity that appropriately challenges your skills (it's not too easy and not too hard) and that often leads to feelings of increased creativity, satisfaction, motivation, and happiness

Fried: a feeling of being tired and overwhelmed as a result of losing your natural curiosity and excitement over things; this happens when your superpower of being Energized has been zapped

Hunchifying: a thinking mistake (a ThoughtHole); when you guess what another person is thinking or how a situation will turn out

Iced: when you decide to not try new things or take chances, because you're afraid of failing or making a mistake; this happens when your superpower of being Resilient has been zapped

Ikigai ("icky guy"): a Japanese word that roughly translates to "the reason why you wake up in the morning"; an idea or belief that shapes one's understanding about what's important in life; a technique for helping you go from Fried to Energized

inner monster: an unkind voice in your head, made up of your own thoughts, that makes you feel bad about yourself by telling you *You're not good enough to be here!* and *You'll never get it right!*

Inner Voice: a thought or feeling inside that lets you know what you like, what you want, and who you are; Inner Voice is the fuel for your superpower of being Original

inside motivation: motivation to do something because you have a natural passion, interest, or curiosity about it—a force that is intrinsic, or from within you (see outside motivation)

laddering: a tool that helps you stop avoiding the person, place, or thing that you're afraid of; you take small steps, one at a time, over a period of time, to expose yourself to the situation or person you are avoiding or worrying about

Lightifying: a thinking mistake (a ThoughtHole); feeling like there is a spotlight turned on you and everyone is judging you in a negative way

loving-kindness: a meditation that involves repeating several statements that are compassionate toward oneself and others, for the purpose of creating feelings of peace and love

Meaning: the value each person personally sees in the things, activities, or relationships around them; a personal opinion on what's important in life; the four things most commonly found to give people meaning in life (as identified by researcher Emily Esfahani Smith) are belonging, purpose, storytelling, and transcendence; Meaning is the fuel for your superpower of being Energized

Mindfulness: paying attention on purpose, in the present moment, and without judgment; Mindfulness is the fuel for your superpower of being Present

mindset: the way you look at the world; by changing your mindset or belief, you can change the feelings you experience inside your body; mindset is the fuel for your superpower of being Resilient

movie theater technique: when you're able to realize that even though you're feeling panicked because things seem scary—when you're watching a movie, for example—you're not in any real danger, and so you can decide that you don't need to feel afraid

noticer: when you're a noticer, you're not trying to change your thoughts; you're just watching or noticing them, which helps create a space between you and your thoughts

optimist: a person who believes that bad things come to an end (temporary), who does not think a challenge in one part of life affects all other parts (specific), and who looks for all the reasons for challenges (externalize)

outside motivation: motivation to do something because you're looking forward to a reward or trying to avoid a punishment—a force that is extrinisic, or from outside you (see inside motivation)

Overlooking: a thinking mistake (a ThoughtHole); when you ignore the positive in a situation and focus only on the negative

pacifying: trying to calm down worrisome thoughts and/or feelings, usually with reassuring verbal messages such as *It's going to be okay*

pessimist: a person who believes that bad things last forever (permanent), who thinks a challenge in one part of life affects every part of life (pervasive), and who blames themselves for challenges (personalize)

ride the wave: a phrase to help you remember that just like a wave, feelings of panic will crash over you and then pass; as you realize that panic is a false alarm, you'll know you're just uncomfortable but totally safe

shoulding: when others give you suggestions about how they think you should behave or feel in order for you to be your best or do your best (see chapter 3)

sleep bubble: a protected space designed to help you sleep well; you activate the sleep bubble by taking certain steps, an hour before bedtime, that will help you fall asleep and get a good night's rest; a technique for helping you go from Fried to Energized

social anxiety: as defined in Superpowered: worrying about what other people think about you; you might worry so much that you even start to avoid certain people or activities

Spam message: you get this message when thinking about the past or the future, or at random times; this message involves recurring thoughts that cause you to worry, yet have no benefit or purpose

squishing: when you ignore your thoughts of worry and pretend they don't exist or you try to make them go away; also known as thought suppression

storytelling: one of the ways for us to share who we are, and a way to see and appreciate the meaning in our lives

Superpowered: when all five of the superpowers you were born with (Present, Original, Whole, Energized, and Resilient) are awake and active

Supersizing: a thinking mistake (a ThoughtHole); making a small challenge much bigger than it really is

SuperVision Glasses: imaginary glasses that help you turn your self-criticisms ("I'm too sensitive") into positive statements about yourself ("I'm good at noticing when a friend needs a hug"); a tool for helping you see your own strengths

ThoughtHoles: thinking mistakes (see Hunchifying, Overlooking, Lightifying, Extremifying, Supersizing)

transcendence: a feeling or state of being when you find yourself in awe, or when you feel totally outside of your normal everyday experience in a positive and inspiring way

What-iffing: when your mind moves out of the present moment and worries about future or past events, frequently asking questions that begin with the phrase "What if . . . ?"; this happens when your superpower of being Present has been zapped

What-iffing dominoes: when one what-if thought is quickly followed by another what-if thought and then another one, and this results in a big story of worry in your mind (see What-iffing)

WOOP: a goal-setting method that helps you overcome challenges you might encounter when working toward a goal; the acronym stands for "Wish, Outcome, Obstacle, Plan"

worry runaround: when you feel worried and it affects all parts of you—your thoughts, feelings, and actions

YETi: an individual who recognizes that it takes time and practice to learn something new (e.g., how to surf) and therefore does not negatively judge their lack of skills; a YETi is careful to say to themselves, "I am not good at this . . . YET!"

zapped: when your superpowers have been forgotten, they've been zapped

RESOURCES

You're still here? Just can't get enough of us, huh? Well, we love you, too, and if you're really looking for more information, we'd be happy to make some recommendations.

GoZen!: Founded by *Superpowered* coauthor Renee Jain, GoZen! uses animation, stories, games, and other materials to teach kids the invaluable skills of resilience. Learn more at GoZen.com.

Dr. Shefali Tsabary: Endorsed by Oprah as revolutionary and life-changing, coauthor Dr. Tsabary's work includes transformative courses, conference experiences, and books on parenting and mindful living. Learn more at DrShefali.com.

VIA Institute on Character: In Superpowered, we reference the twenty-four character strengths that all humans have in different amounts. Discover yours by taking the survey at VIAcharacter.org.

Positive Educator Certification: The PEC program, created by Renee Jain and Emiliya Zhivotovskaya, founder of the Flourishing Center, is a multi-week program that gives teachers the tools to help students cultivate greater resilience, motivation, and well-being. Learn more at PositiveEducator.org.

Master of Applied Positive Psychology: Positive Psychology is the scientific study of the strengths that enable humans and organizations to flourish. Learn more about the Master of Applied Positive Psychology (MAPP) program at the University of Pennsylvania at sas.upenn .edu/lps/graduate/mapp.

ACKNOWLEDGMENTS

We are deeply honored to have been given the opportunity to write this book. To have these pages potentially transform a child's life is a true privilege—one that we don't take lightly.

There are many who helped shape this book into its current form, and we would like to thank each of them.

From Renee:

My mom, dad, and brother, who, no matter what the circumstances, have held a steadfast flame of hope and inspiration in my life.

My love, Shawn, whose feedback enriched the ideas in this book and whose love forever enriches my life.

My kids, Jasmin and Jude, who are my most enlightened and compassionate teachers.

From Shefali's:

My family and friends, most especially my daughter, Maia, who continues to teach, challenge, and inspire me to help myself and other parents become more conscious.

Together, we would like to acknowledge:

Nikki Abramowitz for her brilliant aesthetics through-out the book. Her ideas and boundless talent will help fuel the creative energy within each child.

Lee L. Krecklow for his astute feedback, editing, and incredible disposition that allowed this book to form into its final iteration. His unwavering support and talent have elevated this project by leaps and bounds.

Molly, Sasha, Ashleigh, Eileen, and Kelly—the fabulous GoZen! team—for believing in and supporting this work.

Our incredible clients, who allow us into their homes and hearts. It is because of their courage to be vulnerable that we can do what we do.

Finally, our amazing editor, Sara Sargent, for her clear and focused vision for this book. It is our honor to have given form to that vision on behalf of all the children who will be touched by these pages.

INDEX

ABOUT THE AUTHORS

Annabel L. Lin

Renee Jain, MAPP, is the founder of GoZen! and is recognized as a pioneer in the fields of technology and child psychology. Through her writing, product invention and development, master classes for parents, and advocacy for children, she works to build the emotional intelligence of kids. She holds a masters in psychology and has two children. Find Renee on Twitter at @gozentweets, on Facebook and Instagram at @gozenlove, and online at GoZen.com.

Dr. Shefali Tsabary is a world-renowned clinical psychologist who received her doctorate from Columbia University. She specializes in the integration of Eastern philosophy and Western psychology, making her an expert in her field. She is a frequent keynote speaker who presents at conferences, workshops, and educational and transformational centers around the world. She is raising a teenage daughter. Find Shefali on Twitter @DrShefali, on YouTube and Facebook at DrShefali, and online at DrShefali.com.